P9-DGU-353

Lincoln Christian Colle

The Silent Struggle for Mid-America

Mid-America

The Church in Town and Country Today

THE Silent Struggle for Mid-America

THE CHURCH IN TOWN AND COUNTRY TODAY

E. W. Mueller
and
Giles C. Ekola, Editors

153

Augsburg Publishing House • Minneapolis, Minnesota

THE SILENT STRUGGLE FOR MID-AMERICA

Copyright © 1963 Augsburg Publishing House
All rights reserved
Library of Congress Catalog Card No. 63-16602

Scripture quotations are from the Revised Standard Version of the Bible, copyright 1946 and 1952 by the Division of Christian Education of the National Council of Churches.

MANUFACTURED IN THE UNITED STATES OF AMERICA

FOREWORD

The office of Church in Town and Country of the Division of American Missions of the National Lutheran Council received the request from participating bodies to assist in setting up a study conference to learn what is happening to small towns and the churches in rural areas in Iowa. The response resulted in a significant workshop on "The Church's Concern for Town and Country Communities in Mid-America." The lectures and findings of this important conference make up the contents of this book.

For three days, more than one hundred participants, namely, Lutheran jurisdictional leaders, scholars, and members of church in town and country committees discussed the realities of life in town and country areas of mid-America and the responsibility of the church in the changing situation.

Top-flight sociologists and economists from governmental and private agencies and university faculties drew a sharp and sometimes disturbing picture of the emerging trends in mid-America. Then, against this backdrop, the churchmen diligently sought to identify the issues facing the church in this area of rapid social change.

Small groups spent many hours discussing such subjects as leadership training, effective communication, economic farm problems, purpose for the individual, and Christian goals for family living. Always the basic question was, How can the church help congregations respond in obedience to her Lord in the social situation in which the congregations function?

19531

Pastors and laymen of town and country congregations, mission and jurisdictional administrators, and members of town and country committees, will be stimulated and assisted if they will honestly face reality as it is presented in the first section of this book, identify issues for themselves and act in willing obedience to their Lord.

ROBERT W. LONG

Executive Secretary, Division of American Missions, National Lutheran Council

PREFACE

The wheels of the Milwaukee westbound passenger train came to a screeching stop late one afternoon in December, 1896, at a flag stop on the prairies of South Dakota. A lone figure stepped down into snow that covered the vast plains. The train proceeded westward and was soon out of sight. The lone figure stood like a statue with all his earthly possessions. Books and clothes were held firmly in his grip. There was not a road or path to indicate in what direction he might find shelter or hospitality. Only the train tracks. Westward the tracks stretched into more unknown vastness; eastward, they stretched toward a mission school in southern Germany where he had spent a number of years preparing himself to become a pastor to the immigrants from Europe.

The stillness of the crisp December air was broken by the crunching of snow under horse's feet and under runners of a sled. The man who came to give hospitality to the pastor had not expected the train to be on time.

This perhaps was a part of God's plan because it provided the pastor an excellent setting for the necessary moments to reflect on how his life could be meaningfully invested in the vast emptiness that stretched in all directions. He had come to help establish the church in a new and strange land. This he would do and this he did! After almost fifty years he concluded his ministry in the village in which he began. His ministry had been difficult, steady, and meaningful, but seldom dramatic or sensational.

I tell this story of our prairie pastor because he typifies hundreds of pastors who began their ministry in the great midwest toward the close of the 19th Century; because it indicates the task that confronted the church at that time, namely, to establish the church; and, because it gives us a background for evaluating the church's resources and opportunities in the midwest at this time:

Then people and resources were few; now people and resources are many.

Then facilities were meager and inadequate; now they are adequate and even sometimes pretentious.

Then members were immigrants and strangers in the American community; now members are in the center of community life and many provide community leadership.

Then there were many small denominational groups; now there are major church groups emerging.

Then the groups were strange to each other; now there is coordination of effort and counseling together.

Then the church found it difficult to relate itself to nonchurch groups; now it knows how to use properly the nonchurch resources available to church groups.

Then the task was for the church to establish itself in a new land; now the task is humbly but positively to play the role of a great church in the midst of the rapidly changing social situation of mid-America by ministering meaningfully to a society that is confused:

confused as to what it should counsel its youth as they wrestle with the question of building meaningful lives;

confused as to how to enrich the evening of life that many of its citizens are being privileged to reach;

confused as to what it wants to do with the vast natural resources of the midwest.

This call to give direction to life is indeed a call to greatness. The question is not, does the church have the spiritual and physical resources to answer this call? The question is, will its congregations in mid-America have the courage to answer this call? Or will they be content just to be "successful congregations"?

Congregations will need to be helped, guided, and inspired, but only they, by bearing a personal witness to their faith, can answer the call to greatness.

To help put these concerns into clearer focus was the purpose of the people who planned and who participated in the mid-America workshop.

I wish to express a special word of thanks to the persons who prepared working papers, to those who accepted special assignments in preparation for the workshop, and to those who appeared on the program. We also are indebted to every participant in the workshop.

E. W. MUELLER

CONTENTS

I.

The

Church

Listens

1.

IDENTIFYING FACTORS
IN THE STRUGGLE

A Christian should never be overtaken by change like an unexpected storm in the night. A Christian ought to be the master of change not its victim. But for this to be true the Christian must anticipate the changes that economic and social forces of life set in motion. If our newly emerging society is to be productive for good it needs the intelligent concern and direction of churchmen who will work side by side with experts and exert a Christian influence.

At the beginning of this century programs such as the 4-H Clubs, Future Farmers of America and Extension Service were created to fill the needs of rural people, and these programs were successful in their various intentions. However, these programs were begun at a time when social and educational values were considered secondary to economic ones. In the early decades of this century farming was a long and difficult occupation and success did not come easily. A man's primary concern was for the success of his occupation and to succeed was to sacrifice all other considerations.

In a day when the necessities of life were comparatively difficult to provide and churches were primarily concerned with establishing themselves on new geographical frontiers, it is understandable that economic values were allowed to play so prominent a role.

But today life is far different. We live in a time when the overproduction of things is a major problem. Our church organi-

3

zation is large and complex. Our sons and daughters attend colleges in record numbers and church membership is the highest in our nation's history. Surely noneconomic values need no longer be of secondary importance.

The year 1908 marked a significant accomplishment: the appointment of the first presidential commission on country life. At that time church bodies were hardly more than spectators, but today many pastors are working for a second commission. More important than this, however, is the fact that many Christians are in a position to play a leading role in the stewardship of the town and country community. They can easily forfeit this position if they are content to remain spectators of the agricultural revolution in progress, or they can become actively involved and play a significant role in the building of tomorrow's community.

The Old and the New

Two serious obstacles to the building of this community exist in the attitude of many people toward change itself. Christian churches will have to tear down the altars of two false gods: the deification of the status quo and the deification of newness. Those who worship the status quo thwart adjustments which are necessary and inevitable in a growing and dynamic society. These people do not believe that progress exists in growth and change, but in a precarious preservation of the past. They who wish to preserve the past see change as only a needless tampering with the things they know and love or as a foolhardy gamble. And I am not speaking politically, this worship of the status quo lies above and beyond such political labels as conservative or liberal. It is an even more essential view of life than politics. The people who are committed to the status quo often find the changes they have opposed even more distasteful once they occur. However had these people been less rigid in their demand for no change at all, and had they not refused to take part, they could have exerted a moderating influence upon events.

The church must also destroy the altar built by those who conceive of all change as being progress. Those who want change for the sake of change. Those who indiscriminately believe that every new thing that comes along is better than the last. These are people who have made a shrine out of innovation; who see newness as a merit outranking all others.

Our need for basic concepts of life never changes. We shall always need a sense of integrity; absolute values to guide us in our decisions; a sense of participation in life. But we must find forms of life which transmit these concepts. If we delay too long in this people in their impatience will accept change as progress and will discard their values along with the obsolete forms of life.

It is the price of new tractors and not the love of the old which prevents the farmer from purchasing a new one. But in the area of the church it is often the love of the old building rather than the cost of the new one which causes country folk to delay action. This aptly illustrates a basic issue. The disparity between our acceptance of technology and our reluctance to change familiar institutions. People are such that they will more willingly accept the new advancements of technology and will promptly put the advancements to use. Often because to do so results in some material advantage of money, time or convenience. The rewards are tangible and immediate.

People are slow, however, to accept new ideas and approaches which would involve alterations in the institutional life of a community. The rewards are neither tangible nor immediate and the material advantage seems vague at best. Instead they are confronted by a conflict of values and emotions and they feel a sense of loss.

Thus, technological developments may outdistance the institutional developments in the same community. Technology tends to accelerate change and is forward looking. It creates conflicts, the resolvement of which results in progress. Institutions, on the other hand, resist change and tend to be backward looking. This creates conflicts which lead to decline and frustration. This situation leaves us with institutions which were designed to serve a community which no longer exists due to the changes wrought by technology.

The Farm and the Church

There is nothing sacred about the family farm as an economic unit, but there is something sacred about the family. A farm, quite simply as a family's home, merits our concern. There is nothing sacred about what kind of a farm a man may have, or how large or small it may be, but the man who does the farming is important. There is something sacred about the human personality and we must be concerned for the way people live.

The Christian concept of work demands that a man find significant meaning and satisfaction in his labor. The complexity of industrial life with its intricate web of assembly line and increasing specialization obscures this satisfaction for many of us. Consequently such concepts as man, family, community and work must be clearly redefined in order that their relation to conditions of present-day life are understood.

People need a workable philosophy that is rooted in their Maker to guide them in their daily decisions. Such a philosophy is essential if the values and religious beliefs of people are to be evident in their actions. The existence of a philosophy of life based on man's dependence and responsibility to a Divine Providence has a direct bearing on our future. We are discovering how difficult it is to deal with nations which have repudiated God. Yet we often act as though God were not concerned in all of the areas of our life. Our constitution separates church and state and quite wisely. But this does not mean that God is not concerned with the conduct of our society nor does it remove it from his province. Christian values are essential to the good conduct of our society and to fail to realize this is to fail in our responsibility as Christians. We seem to proceed under the assumption that honesty, integrity in one's work, respect for man and God, are all so priceless that they will perpetuate themselves. Values procured at great cost will survive only if succeeding generations are willing to spend equal effort to protect and transmit them. And the best way to transmit these values is to make them so integral a part of our everyday life that they are constantly reflected in what we do.

Much is being done to give people all the knowledge and resources necessary to cope with the crises we are facing, but not enough is being done to restate our values and beliefs so that their relevancy is apparent in the development of possible solutions. Because of the failure to restate our values adequately for our own day, people make the naive assumption that their beliefs and values are not relevant to the solutions they seek and they are thus unduly influenced by temporal issues.

The question is not whether our beliefs and values have relevancy to our problems, but whether we permit our values to shape our decisions. Do we translate our values into a God-centered workable philosophy? Do we expend enough effort in identifying the role our values should have in shaping the future of our community? Do theologians for each generation adequately restate basic Christian concepts so they continue to give meaning and purpose to life?

Our failure to deal with these questions has resulted in a host of problems. The wholeness of life has been destroyed as all sorts of various creeds and persuasions are deified and raised to an all-powerful, all-conclusive status. Politics, economics, science, humanitarianism, the variety is as great as the enthusiasm of their supporters. The disciples of these creeds overwhelm us with the rhetoric of their cause. They promise solutions to all our problems if we but acknowledge the omnipotence of their favorite. Yet, to deify one system of ideas, results in a conflict with the others. Different kinds of knowledge were designed to work in harmony with one another to serve man in his struggle for advancement, but they become man's downfall when they are exalted to the rank of a god. No creed or persuasion has the power of God and consequently to deify one is to have it challenged by another, and so in a state of confusion we stumble from one "ism" to another and from one set of slogans to the next.

People fail to act responsibly when they universalize the object of their responsibility, and are responsible for no one in particular. The individual cannot transfer the responsibility for his acts to the organization to which he belongs. God does not hold the organization responsible: he holds responsible the individuals who make up the organization. Our concern is that our values and religious beliefs be brought into the process by which we make decisions.

Armed with biblical concepts laymen must be encouraged and supported to bear witness in policy-making groups; groups whose decisions will determine the character of our communities. In our mass society, action is initiated by organizations or groups of organizations. A lone man can have little direct influence on trends. But he can make his influence felt in the organization to that he belongs and the organization in turn can influence the shape of things to come.

We assume as a nation that man is responsible for what he does and that his acts are judged by God. We further assume that this means more than a moralistic evaluation with a *general* responsibility for the well-being of society. The *universal* human which unites us with all of mankind serves as a mere philosophical screen behind which people can hide from acting responsibly for their real neighbor.

Jesus took another position. He emphasized that we act responsibly in word and deed. My neighbor is always an individual for whom I am personally responsible and who conversely is responsible for me. The categories of good and evil presuppose a sense of obligation which is meaningful only if man lives in relationship to a God who cannot be impressed by beauty, economic laws, mechanical necessity, or claims of social complexity.

The Church in Mid-America

The church was brought to mid-America by circuit riders, frontier pastors and the many pious immigrants who came to this area, and the consequent structure of the church was the existence of many small congregations. In 1920 the average membership for a village church was 144, and for a church in the open country 84 members. These small congregations lacked sufficient funds to carry out their accepted functions. They had difficulty attracting good leaders and had trouble maintaining an influence upon their youth. And despite their reputation for friendliness and warm-hearted cordiality, they tended to be clannish and failed to reach effectively those in the community who had no church.

This superabundance of rural churches was causing difficulty before the impact of the agricultural revolution was felt, as is evident from the 1909 report of the Commission on Country Life. Further the depression of the thirties put a financial strain on many struggling congregations. The rural exodus of the forties due to the war and the war industries decreased the membership roles of many congregations. This situation was not reversed by the end of the war, but was accelerated by the increased use of technology.

Still the situation is not completely negative. Many congregations have made necessary adjustments and though these have not been made without emotional tensions and sometimes sadness, these realignments and consolidations have generally strengthened the churches concerned. The church structure of many communities has been altered. Churches which once were landmarks in the countryside are now empty or gone. Still other churches, once small and modest, are now thriving. These changes do not represent the capitulation of the church to a whimsical fate, but signify the ability of the church to adapt itself to changing communities to serve the needs of its people.

Yet, we speak of this period of transition as the magnificent decline of the church in town and country. As a result of the agricultural revolution, we find ourselves with fewer churches but with better programs, better leadership and a decreasing number of unchurched people in the community. An organized and planned effort on the part of the local church leaders is helping congregations to make the necessary adjustments. The total result will be fewer churches but better churches—churches which have the capacity to bring a more adequate ministry to their community.

The church is not a rigid, inflexible institution. Rather it is responsive to the needs of men and may change to minister better to the community which it serves. As Dean Louis Almen points out later in this volume, religion ought never be identified with any particular social arrangement or particular set of customs.

The church cannot identify itself with either geography or buildings. A church's location, or name, or architecture are all secondary to the needs of the people it is to serve. Thus the emphasis is placed on the interrelatedness and interdependence of the people in village, town, open country and small city. The church's position in town and country is a potentially strong one and this strength can be used to exert a Christian influence. However as our rural areas experience far-reaching socioeconomic change, major adjustments are necessary and these in turn involve major decisions.

Changes in methods of farming have set into motion two very significant population movements. One is the rapid decline of the farm population and the other is the growth of the rural nonfarm population. These shifts often occur simultaneously in the same community.

People are living in the country community, but they are dependent upon economic opportunities other than agriculture. In some cases industry has moved into the community. In others, improved transportation has made urban employment accessible. In yet other cases urbanites have become weary of congested living and have taken advantage of improved transportation to move to the country.

Thus rural communities are losing their homogeneous nature
and often people living in the same community have nothing
in common but geographical space. The only time neighbors
may meet is at some public function or at the stores where they
shop. The image of the closely-knit farm community, bound together by common problems and successes has become an anach-
ronism. In areas that undergo a decline of population, distance
itself is a social liability and churches and schools stand empty.

The Silent Struggle

Thus, gradually the hidden struggle in mid-America mutely
reveals itself. Occasionally it may come to public attention as
in the holding action of the National Farmer's Organization or
in the publicity given to the Wheat Referendum, but largely
it is a silent conflict of unexpressed antagonisms and unspoken
grievances. Of the problems confronting American society the
rural dilemma is probably the least known and the least understood. This is partly due to the almost inherent apathy of an
overwhelmingly urban population without adequate means of
understanding or relating rural circumstances. But just as much,
perhaps, it is due to the confusion of the farmer himself as to
what he ought to do. The farmer's seeming inability to frame
his problems clearly and logically so that possible solutions become apparent. This, the farmer has not yet done. In fact, he
has barely begun to define realistically the problems which he
faces. Further, the emotional implications of the situation com-
pound the confusion and impede objectivity. Various solutions
have been proposed by the federal government and by private
organizations, but the diversity of their programs and the differences of their theories make elementary agreement almost impossible and the stalemate continues.

When farmers have an opportunity to express themselves,
their problems and frustrations become apparent. They are
bothered by the meagerness of their financial returns and the
increasing demands for investment capital. They are unable

to provide for their families as they want to. Also they cannot spend enough time with their families when their workweek throughout the year averages well over fifty hours. Changes in the community seem to rob rural life of many of its advantages. Financial conditions often preclude a son from following in his father's occupation and children move to the city for work in increasing numbers. And perhaps above all, the stability and certainty that once marked life in the country seems gone.

2.

CHRISTIAN COMMUNITY
AND CITIZEN COMMUNITY

Only the sociologist or the psychologist is in a real position to learn what actually motivates people toward their decisions. The theologian is more likely to suggest what *ought* to guide them if they receive their basic motivations from the Christian tradition. He may supplement this theoretical criterion with knowledge gained from general observation, available studies in motivation, and intuition, but he cannot be sure that what he says is true or only wishful thinking.

With this acknowledgment of my particular weakness concerning the subject at hand, I will attempt to describe the relationships between the Christian community and the citizen community. I choose this terminology carefully in order to avoid some of the more insensitive vocabulary often used, such as sacred and secular, or holy and profane, or church (with the emphasis upon the institution) and state (meaning governmental offices). This language may be quite appropriate on the right occasion. The points I wish to make lend themselves more readily to the terms, Christian community and citizen community.

By Christian community I mean, of course, the church. The church is most easily observed in its institutional form, but we are misled if we believe that this is its primary or even its most functional form. The church in the Protestant tradition is the community. All the basic Protestant confessions define the

13

church in similar language—the church is the communion of saints (or Christian community) in which the Gospel is preached and the sacraments administered. This is the basic meaning for the Roman Catholic as well. The institutional form through which this community seeks to express itself may and does vary, but this form is to a large degree irrelevant as far as the essential nature of the community is concerned. (Here the Roman Catholic would tend to disagree, although perhaps not as much as is commonly supposed by Protestants.)

By citizen community, I mean that vast array of routine and complex sets of human relationships in which every person participates. It includes family, job, school, play, and local, state, national, and international categories. It has aspects we call race, class, economic levels, emotional planes, age, sex, education, opportunity, geography, time, and health.

I do not mean to suggest by this distinction that the two communities are mutually exclusive or even easily distinguishable. Part of the problem is that they are very nearly completely intermingled. The Christian is a citizen also within his Christian community. He cannot easily separate the two in either function or thought. The citizen who is not in the Christian community cannot escape being influenced by it (at least in this society) even to the extent of having adopted some of its basic tenets that in turn determine his decision-making.

The Christian Community

Let us examine the Christian community first, attempting a description of its basic character. This community, first of all, shares every aspect of any ordinary understanding of community. It consists of people of a particular time and place who share in the environmental features of their age. They occupy a spot in history which shapes by accident (or design) certain presuppositions which govern their view of themselves and the world. Western men, for example, have inherited certain views from the Greco-Roman civilization that sometimes dominate their thinking. A twentieth century man has the age of science to influence him as well as a host of other pressures peculiar to this era of mankind.

A simple definition of community is that it is a set of personal interrelationships which are created by common interests, beliefs and values. A community is bound together by shared convictions made by experience or accident. The community is a community only so long as these certain values produce the adhesive quality peculiar to the particular community.

The Christian community is, therefore, a thoroughly human community. To the Christian this means, in his language, that it is a sinful community. The weaknesses, prejudices, and mistakes common to all men are as much a part of the Christian community as any community. The idea that the Christian is holy while others are unholy must be very carefully understood. A Christian is holy only because he lives within a community where God is working in a particular way and because he believes he has received forgiveness for his sins. He is not necessarily a better man than the non-Christian. Indeed, it is quite possible that he may *not* be at any particular stage of his life or understanding. Nor does he claim greater wisdom than his non-Christian fellow citizen. He claims only the gift of trust in God.

But second, we must quickly add that the Christian community is not wholly understood by its purely human aspects. It believes that it is also a divine community. It is human and divine at the same time. This language is intended to convey the belief that the Christian community is that place where God chooses to lead and guide those who have responded to him in faith. Through the preaching and witnessing of the Gospel and the receiving of the sacraments, a community is created which transcends the historical and temporal limitations of the purely human community. The Holy Spirit is active and men are committed to certain beliefs which are quite different from those outside this community.

The basic belief is that at a time and place God acted in a cosmic way to change the course of history and to insure the ultimate victory of love and justice. To this event we give the name Jesus Christ. Furthermore, God continues to act through certain means to lead and guide his people through the great crises of life to a great goal which lies beyond history.

This paradoxical combination of divinity and humanity is not easily observable by the nonmember. Certain aspects of it are discernible, such as works of love, devotion to certain values, particular habits of life, worship, etc., but its essential realities are not available to the sociologist or even the psychologist.

A third point in this connection which is quite important to the Protestant understanding is that this community is most adequately defined in terms of that which brings it into being rather than in terms of what it is. The church is a community *in which* the Gospel is preached. The relative clause is determinative. The church is a community whose basic orientation is understood in terms of what happens there and not how it exhibits itself. A church is not a Christian community because it holds certain confessions, or performs rites in a certain way, or has certain buildings. The church is the church when the community which it is, is created by, gathers around and perpetuates the message from God in Christ. Churches, speaking institutionally, which appear to be churches may not, in fact, be so. It is actual preaching of the Christian message which determines their reality.

This has a lot to say about the relationships among the various Christian institutions. A Protestant believes (or ought to believe) that the church is wherever the love and justice of God in Christ are preached and believed. He may shun particular kinds of fellowship with other churches because he believes that the Gospel is subverted or compromised; but at the same time, he believes that there is only one God manifest in many communal forms of which his is only one.

Lastly, the Christian community is understood in terms of a paradoxical relationship between individual and community. The value of the individual is incalculable. He makes his own decisions, comes into the community as an individual, receives and exercises his freedom as an individual. But he believes that at the same time he is part of a complex of relationships that he calls a community. He is free only as he is part of this community. The community comes before him and goes on after him. He becomes a true person only within the context of this community. This is an extremely important value for him because it underscores his uniqueness and integrity at the same time that it produces confidence and varied avenues of expression.

The Citizen Community

Seen from the Christian's point of view, the citizen community is not a great deal different *for him*. The same God who called him through the Gospel message also rules the world. The Christian exercises his existence in his citizen experiences and his salvation relationships in the same time and place. Justice and love are a part of this citizen communal world, too. The primary difference is that God does not exercise his lordship through grace in this "outside" community but through justice. God comes to men to "save" them within the Christian community. He exercises his will through the citizen community to achieve justice, peace, and welfare. Whether or not the non-Christian citizen shares the Christian ideas concerning man's ultimate goals, he is subject to the same reason, the same fears, the same difficulties, and the same needs. Even though the Christian God may not be recognized in the citizen community, the Christian feels responsible to call upon all men to exercise their lives according to the knowledge which they have without direct revelation from God.

The Christian believes that the world is a battleground of good and evil, and this includes, of course, the church. In this predicament of conflicting forces, he believes that the good judgment of discerning men provides sufficient foundation for a just society, in whatever form the particular time and place may require. Certain structures are evident—the family unit, the equality of man's rights, the necessity of peaceful arbitration of honest differences, a coercive force to restrict and punish evil. The Christian also believes in change and development, for just as his Christian community is flexible enough to live in its day, so his citizen community changes and grows, recedes and learns.

The Christian views the integrity of the individual in the citizen community in the same way as he views it in his Christian community. And he understands the responsibility that the individual has for the whole as well. The binding beliefs of the citizen community are the same as in the Christian community to the degree that they encompass the necessity of justice, the well-being of all men, and the freedom to subdue the earth and harness it for human welfare.

The Relationships Between the Two Communities

With this basic theory behind us, we can sketch an outline of the nature of the relationships between the two communities. Since we have defined the church as a viable entity of actual practicing beliefs and personal relationships, a description of its relationships to the citizen community, a similar entity, is not easy to encompass. The relationships lie on a personal plane, rather than on generalities. It is obvious that a relationship already exists in the very essence of the Christian community in the citizen community. The Christian has a relationship to the society around him, without *doing* anything. He exists in the citizen community willy nilly. Our question is not whether or not a relationship exists, but how it is to be exercised. And it is here that the values and beliefs, which constitute faith, are all-determinative. It is precisely these which lead the Christian to the ways and means that he, in his personal and communal life, forms and carries out his life in the world.

There are two beliefs which govern his attitude. The first we can call simply the doctrine of creation. The Christian believes that this is God's world, created by him and created good. The antithesis between materialism and spiritualism is unchristian. This is a typical Greek way of thinking and permeates our western civilization, but is foreign to the Hebrew-Christian tradition. Man's body is not bad and his spirit good. Rather, the Christian says that his body and soul are one entity, and they are both (one can omit "both") bad in the sense that they have not achieved their ultimate perfection. He, body and soul, is a sinner, limited in his capacity, fallen short of his goal, by his very nature in this present stage of history inclined to subvert the divine categories of love and justice.

The Christian's goal is not to escape this world. He is rather to live in it, be a disciple in it, until God's purposes find fulfillment for him in another setting. He is, indeed, to love this world, even as Christ loved it, and to give himself to it, as Christ did. He is not to love it above God, but to love it as God loves it. This simple concept illumines the foundation for man's every action in the world. Many, many Christians have not understood it and have instead followed a more Greek way of thinking of the world as illusory and secondary in its reality. The prophets of the Old Testament would have been amazed. They, after all, wrote Genesis.

To the Christian, it follows that the power structures of the world are not bad. They have evil lurking in them, even as the Christian himself does, but they are not by their nature evil. The Christian is to use them for good ends rather than evil ends. Labor unions or the N.F.O. do not violate the Christian view of the world by using power. Neither is National Defense questionable at this stage of our thinking. Coercive power must be used in this fallen world. It is the nonuse or misuse of it which is disobedience to God.

A further implication is that the world is to be lived in now. Salvation, in the biblical sense, is not "pie in the sky by and by" but *now*. The future belongs to God and the Christian trusts him for it. The present, in a very real sense, belongs to him, the Christian, and it is here that his real concerns must be expressed.

This leads us to the second basic belief, which we usually call

stewardship. This means the responsibility that falls to a man
who believes in God to obey God as he lives in the world. A
Christian is responsible for his society, as well as for his children and his church. He does not leave the use of the power
structures to other men. This is more eminently his responsibility than any other. The exercise of this stewardship, however,
involves him in many problems.

There are two basic ways he exercises his responsibility: as
an individual and as part of a community. As an individual,
he participates in the citizen community with full abandon. He
suffers with and seeks to solve the social and political concerns of his fellow non-Christian citizen. He does not condemn
the world, but the evil in it. He understands his own lack of
wisdom and recognizes that often his non-Christian brother has
more wisdom than he in working through the problem. (He
can, for example, vote for a non-Christian over a Christian for
public office with good conscience if he feels the non-Christian
is better qualified and has better convictions than the Christian.)
He discovers, for example, that he often agrees more with
the methodology of a non-Christian than with a fellow Christian. He may engage in a freedom ride to the consternation of
his fellow Christian and the joy of his humanitarian non-Christian. And he discovers that his reputation for "holiness" is tar-
nished by his actions. This is a risk he accepts. For participation in the world results in suffering, even from the hands of
his own. He recalls that Jesus was called a wine-bibber and a
charlatan because he associated with tax-collectors and pros-
titutes. If his beliefs and values are firm, they carry the day for
him, not social approval.

In his works in the world, he does not claim greater wisdom.
But he claims to seek the will of God. This will of God is not
used as a club over others, which is so tempting, but as the
source of strength for his own actions. He is willing to learn
through his mistakes, knowing that his own actions are often
tainted with wrong motivations and sometimes weakened by
the ambiguity of his own convictions. But he acts nevertheless,

for he is responsible to God to act. His actions sometimes are passive, depending upon time and circumstance (take the East German Christian as an example), but they are calculated and conscious.

Action within his community, the church, is, in many ways, a more troublesome matter. In our pluralistic society, the multiplicity of the Christian communities creates problems not often faced in the history of Christianity. The precedents are few and sometimes unhappy. I think it is safe to say that the Christian community in this country has not yet learned the most effective way it can carry out its stewardship toward the citizen community. And I think that is how it ought to be expressed—stewardship of the community. The community itself is like an individual (an image of the church in the New Testament is a mature man) and has basically the same beliefs and problems that the individual has. The Christian community is as responsible to the citizen community as are its individual members. The same values apply.

But how is the Christian community to exercise this stewardship? One of its great problems is the multiplicity of opinion. If each individual member has the freedom to decide methods of working within his values and beliefs, how can the community act as an individual in terms of being one in purpose? The answer is that it cannot always. The Christian community is diverse—this is its freedom and its glory—it is bound together in such a way that each one is free. In many ways, the Christian community mirrors its own society in this respect. Yet the Christian community must act, if it is to be responsible. Its consensus must come with time, as interest, discussion, and learning combine to produce sometimes remarkable consensus. Sometimes (perhaps much too often) the lack of consensus leads to quietism, when it ought to lead to further intensification to find a consensus. At other times, it leads to superficial consensus, when, for example, church officials pretend to speak for their communities when they actually do not.

Yet there are guidelines for action. The church is, first of all, a conscience for its society. It acts as one who stands apart from society and judges it, not in the sense of condemning, but in the sense of constructive criticism. This is always the role of conscience, even in the individual. In doing so, it, of course, judges itself for it is a part of the society it seeks to serve. A second image is that of the mustard seed or the salt. It deliberately seeks to permeate society with its values and beliefs through witness and action so that the whole society acts in concert with the church's ultimate aims. It holds up the picture of the ultimate goals, even though it has not attained these within its own community. It is therefore a teacher, not in the sense of being all wise, but in the sense of having experienced, and therefore having earned, the right to speak with the other voices.

But it does not end there. It must act in concert action. The ways are many. The weakest is, perhaps, in terms of resolutions passed by democratic process in the Christian community. Enormously helpful at times, these are very often superficial. At other times, it can use its persuasive power for specific actions, such as actions to arouse the citizenship to exercise its proper coercive power in the local community. It may endorse the social improvement movements in the society through its own active membership in them. It can serve as arbitrator, under certain circumstances, of the conflicts of the power structures.

In these actions, the Christian community must remember that it cannot use the power of the sword. This belongs to the citizen community. The Christian community uses "spiritual weapons" of persuasion, witness, and passive resistance.

A second great problem for the Christian community in its communal actions is that it runs the danger of either becoming the tool of unscrupulous elements in the citizen community or becoming identified with elements which it actually opposes. I say this as frankly as I can: The Christian community must run this risk. To retreat from it is a denial of its stewardship. It will burn its fingers, it will make mistakes, it will be embarrassed and even persecuted, but it *must* run the risk. Only by running the risk can it learn, and only through probing actions can it produce a consensus for itself.

In the great town and country problems of this decade, for example, the church, both city and rural, has lagged far behind other progressive elements in the society in influence and help. My job is not to suggest the actual ways it should help. I would have to know much more about each individual proposal to be responsible in such opinions; but I do make the judgment that as I see the church in the great middle west, I do see for the most part, a church identified with only segments of the society, only aspects of the problems, aloof, and even with an attitude of disdain. The church must learn to be both withdrawn and fully involved if it is to perform its function of somewhat objective judgment and responsible action.

The church is a community where the Gospel is preached and where men respond in faith. This is the way that the church is a community which is bound together by the values and beliefs of God's revelation in Christ. But the church is also in the world, responsible for and dedicated to God's will for the world. To step aside from man's problems in social and political spheres is to abdicate the Gospel itself and become no church.

3.

COMMERCIAL FARMING
IN THE CORN BELT

Commercial farming is one of the greatest success stories in America. The rural farm population, as counted in the 1960 census, amounts to just 7.5 per cent of the total population. This small group of people not only adequately feeds and clothes the 185 million people in the United States, but also produces considerable agricultural surplus for export. The bulk of society has been freed from the task of working the land in order to feed themselves. Less than 80 years ago, half the population was required on farms to feed this nation. Without this success in farming, our present level of living in the United States could not be maintained. We have been able to enjoy a high level of consumption of agricultural products, maintain industrial and military growth, and even have a surplus of commodities for export.

Total farm output increased approximately 2.2 per cent per year during the 1940's and approximately 2.5 per cent per year during the 1950's. What has caused this rate of increase in agricultural production? During the past two decades revolutionary changes have taken place in farming methods and production. The rapid increase in demand and prices during World War II and in the immediate postwar years provided economic incentive for farmers to accelerate adoption of improved production practices which were based on research developed during the inter-war period. The shift from animal power to tractor power was an important source of increase in farm output in the 1940's. From 1940 to 1960 the number of farm trucks and tractors per farm unit has almost doubled. This shift not only increased efficiency but released acres formerly required to produce feed for animals.

Increased crop production per acre has been a dominant feature in the growth of farm production since 1940. Crop yields per acre increased 60 per cent from 1940 to 1960. Favorable cost-price relationships throughout the period were an important stimulant to increased use of yield improving practices. Commercial fertilizers, for example, were the largest single factor in the expansion of total crop production. The amount of fertilizer used per farm unit nearly trebled between 1940 and 1960. Greater use of improved varieties of crops also contributed significantly to increased production. An outstanding example is hybrid corn which raised yields per acre about 20 per cent compared with the use of open-pollinated varieties of seed. A greatly expanded production of feed crops provided the basis for a one-third increase in livestock production from 1940 to 1955. Both number of animal breeding units and production per animal rose greatly.

What, then, about the future? Much of the technological revolution which has occurred in agriculture since 1940 is the direct result of the research and extension work of the land-grant colleges and the USDA. In spite of the fact that the proportion of federal governmental appropriations for research which are devoted to agricultural research are becoming much smaller and the fact that both agricultural research and extension are experiencing difficulties in obtaining increased appropriations in a majority of the states, it seems safe to predict that innovations will continue. Private firms are engaging in agricultural research activities to a larger extent. Individual farmers now have a higher level of management ability and training and operate in an economic framework which rewards higher production. It is estimated that by 1975 average farmers will be obtaining yields which are now obtained with the best current research and extension information.

A recent USDA analysis of the future, "Land and Water—A Policy Guide," indicates our 1980 food and fiber needs could be met with some 50 million acres less cropland than we had in 1959. A net increase of some 13 million acres for pasture, range, and forest land was projected, but this need can easily be met. Thus we could release millions of acres from agricultural use by 1980, export one-third more than in 1960, and still provide a more desirable diet for the increased population of 260 million Americans.

A second major issue is the relative rate of growth of farm production and population. Population growth in the last two decades has been between 1.5 and 1.8 per cent per year. At the present time, the total production of agriculture is out-distancing the rate of population growth by more than 0.5 per cent per year. The peculiar nature of demand for agricultural products intensifies the problem. The individual stomach is only so large and the individual back is only so broad. When the basic desires for food and fiber are satisfied, we are unwilling to pay more for additional food and fiber. On the other hand, if we have one car we frequently will be willing to pay about the same for a second car. In fact, many families in the United States now have two or three cars. The situation is similar for air conditioners, radios, television sets, and other consumer goods.

This ability to produce more than is demanded at a reasonable price has led to a serious price-cost disparity for farmers. Since the 1947-49 period, the average price of agricultural commodities has fallen approximately 12 per cent. The average price paid for commodities used in production has risen approximately 12 per cent. Even if farmers have furnished the consumer and industry with farm commodities at 12 per cent lower prices, other parts of the economy have increased their prices of production cost items to the farmer 12 per cent, cutting his profits a total of 24 per cent.

Commercial Farms Are Getting Larger

The size of Corn Belt commercial farms has been increasing steadily. From 1947-49 to 1960, the hog-dairy farm has increased from 158 to 178 acres, hog-beef fattening farms from 192 to 216 acres, and cash-grain farms from 222 to 248 acres (Table 1). A corresponding increase has taken place in gross income. The hog-dairy farm has increased from $9,956 gross income to $11,939 during the period 1947-49 to 1960. Similar percentage increases have occurred in the hog-beef and cash grain farms. Coupled with this trend toward larger commercial farms has been the trend toward fewer farms. The number of farms and commercial farms in the Corn Belt has been decreasing steadily. From 1950 to 1954 the number of farms in the Corn Belt region decreased 67,013 or 7.2 per cent.[1] This is an average of about 13,400 farms per year. Since 1954 the decrease has continued.

It would seem this trend toward larger farms will continue for some time. The gross income figures for "average" farms given above are very near the minimum "adequate" size farm business. It has been suggested that an "adequate" size farm business now should yield at least $10,000 gross income. This size will vary by state and type of farm depending upon the factor cost and organizational pattern. However, in 1954 fewer than 30 per cent of the commercial farms in the Corn Belt region had gross incomes above $10,000, and while the 1959 census data have not been tabulated for the Corn Belt, the percentage probably is not much higher. Thus, many farmers have great incentive for increasing their size of business, especially in areas where the operator can gain control of more resources and increase his net income.

Increased Capital Requirements

The increase in production per farm has been associated with similar large increases in the volume of capital used in pro-

Table I. Comparison of Selected Items on Corn Belt Farms, 1947-49 and 1960

Item	Unit	Hog-Dairy		Hog-Beef Fattening		Cash-Grain	
		1947-49	1960	1947-49	1960	1947-49	1960
Land in farm	Acres	158	178	192	216	222	248
Gross farm income	Dollars	9,956	11,939	19,182	23,221	13,732	15,159
Total farm capital	Dollars	33,700	56,240	50,920	83,370	58,220	109,670
Net farm income	Dollars	5,386	4,616	10,343	5,422	8,802	6,780
1960 net farm income as a per cent of 1947-49		(86)		(52)		(77)	
Return per $100 invested	Dollars	7.90	0.49	14.61	1.41	11.70	3.33
Return per hour of family	Dollars	1.10	.31	2.22	.07	2.21	.02

Source: "Farm Costs and Returns, Commercial Farms by Type, Size, and Location," Agricultural Information Bul. No. 23, USDA, ERS, June 1961.

duction. Total production per unit of capital is only slightly higher than it was in the early 1940's. This means the commercial farmer has been able to increase his production by increased use of capital. The total capital of a hog-dairy farm has increased from approximately $34,000 in 1947-49 to approximately $56,000 in 1960. The hog-beef fattening farm capital has increased from $51,000 to $83,000 and the cash-grain farm capital from $58,000 to $110,000.

A look at the resource requirements for specified operator or labor management incomes provides another perspective of capital required in farming.[2] On a hog-beef farm in southern Iowa, it is estimated that approximately $43,000 investment capital is required to obtain annual operator earnings of $2,500. If annual operator earnings of $5,500 is the goal, $89,000 in investment capital is required. Operator earnings of $2,500 for a southeastern Minnesota dairy farm would require $42,000 investment capital, and earnings of $5,500 would require $73,000 investment capital. In contrast to these present and projected capital requirements, the amount of capital invested in manufacturing is only $15,300 per worker.

The increasing amount of capital needed for larger farms is likely to have far-reaching effects on the structure of an industry like agriculture. In the past new capital in agriculture has been formed almost entirely from earnings within the industry and largely by the operator himself. What will be the future methods of obtaining this capital?

There is evidence that some new types of farm financing are developing. "Vertical coordination," where capital for agricultural production is largely furnished outside of agriculture by an integrator, is an example. However, banks and other traditional credit sources, both public and private, are aware of the increasing capital needs, and as the size of the farm business expands, they are making larger loans. There is little evidence of a significant movement toward large corporate farming as a means of obtaining outside capital.

Lower Returns

The disparity between costs and prices and the increasing capital requirements have led to sharply lowered returns for Corn Belt farms. Net farm income in 1960 was 86 per cent of the 1947-49 average for the hog-dairy farm, 52 per cent of the 1947-49 average for the hog-beef fattening farm, and 77 per cent of the 1947-49 average for the cash-grain farm. But preliminary estimates of net farm income for 1961 are significantly higher for all three types of farms.

The net farm income for average Corn Belt farms might lead to the assumption that farmers are doing fairly well. The incomes range from $4,800 to $7,600. However, if we look at the return per $100 invested after a charge has been made for family and operator labor at hired wage rates, or at the return per hour of family labor after a charge has been made for use of capital, the situation is quite different. The return per $100 invested has fallen from $7.90 in 1947-49 to 49 cents (0.5 per cent) in 1960 for the hog-dairy farm. The return per $100 invested on the hog-beef farm has fallen from $14.61 in 1947-49 to $1.41 (1.4 per cent) in 1960. The return on the cash-grain farm has fallen from $11.70 in 1947-49 to $3.33 (3.3 per cent) in 1960. If it were possible many farmers would be better off to liquidate their assets at current value, put the money in a savings account at 4 per cent, and work in town.

The return per hour of labor on the hog-dairy farms has traditionally been low, $1.10 per hour in 1947-49, and 31 cents in 1960. Large reductions also have occurred on the hog-beef fattening farm and the cash-grain farm. The return per hour on the hog-beef farm was $2.22 per hour in 1947-49 and 2 cents in 1960.

These figures present a very dismal picture for farming in the Corn Belt. Why then do farmers stay in farming, why do other farmers attempt to get started, and why do farmers attempt to expand the size of their farm? First, these are average figures; many alert, progressive farmers do much better than the average.

Second, if a farmer were to sell his farm, he would have a sizable gain of assets. He would have to pay tax on this gain and thus the cost of converting his assets into cash would be considerable. This increase in the value of assets is not included in the net income figures. The farmer who bought his farm twenty years ago has had, in some instances, annual capital gains in the value of the assets almost equal to the average net income. Also, the addition of land and equipment to increase the size of farm is a method for the farmer to raise his absolute net income and oftentimes his rate of return.

Growing Specialization

Farms in the Corn Belt have commonly carried several enterprises in the past. However there has been a definite trend toward product specialization in recent years.

The number of enterprises per farm for the United States dropped from 5.4 in 1940 to 4.7 in 1954. An estimate for 1959 is 3.8 enterprises per farm. Many farmers have eliminated small enterprises for home-use, such as the family milk cow, or a small flock of chickens. At the same time, farmers have found it profitable to specialize in commercial production of a relatively few enterprises, frequently to better utilize the large capital investments and special management abilities.

Along with the growing specialization of farmers has been the trend toward increased utilization of supplies produced off the farm. Farming itself can now be called a "nonfarm input industry." More than half of the materials used in agriculture now come from nonfarm sources. The proportion of nonfarm materials has increased from about a third of total materials in 1940 to more than half currently. Roughly 8 per cent of the people in the United States live on farms, and they buy a quarter of all the trucks sold, use more gasoline than any other industry, and provide a major market for steel, rubber, and chemicals. With continued development of new technology, we will probably see a continuation of the trend toward specialization and the use of more nonfarm materials. This trend will require ever increasing management ability.

Decreasing Opportunities for Getting Established in Farming

A situation related to the above and deserving special comment is the decreasing opportunity for getting established in farming.[3] Getting established in farming means more than getting started. It means achieving security of tenure on a farm with an adequate volume of business, exercising a major degree of managerial control, and acquiring sufficient equity in farm operating capital. As farms in the Corn Belt grow larger, more mechanized in operation, and more specialized in productive organization, the problem of getting started and getting established is largely one of meeting higher requirements in land, capital, and management.

The opportunities for beginning farmers have been limited in recent years. In the ten-year period, 1945-54, only 16 per cent of the farms in the 13 North Central states became available to beginning farmers. Although 31 per cent of the farms were vacated by retiring farmers, 15 per cent were used for enlargement. At these rates, farming opportunities were available for only a third of the boys born on farms. The remaining two-thirds entered nonfarm occupations.

One-man farms may easily require a tenant investment of $15,000 not including land, if labor is to be efficiently utilized. Finding an adequate size farm is a primary problem, especially for an aspiring beginning farmer without family ties to available land. The leasing arrangement is vital to starting farmers. Both crop share leases and livestock share leases may be useful if the terms meet the requirements of the beginning farmer and the landlord. Family ties are also an important source of operating capital although normal credit channels, wisely used, may be adequate.

The difficulty of getting established in farming is likely to increase rather than decrease in the future. Many families are making great efforts to remain in farming and to enlarge their farms. They are using their savings and credit available to compete with other established farms and beginning farmers for land. Thus, the capital required for getting established in farming, especially if land ownership is involved, will continue to grow. Also, the requirements for food and fiber in the decades ahead will be met with a decreasing amount of labor. The difficulty of getting established, plus the low returns in agriculture, will lead many young farm people into nonfarm jobs.

The Family Farm

The family farm has been a strong and stable institution in the Corn Belt. Is the family farm threatened by the trend toward larger more specialized farms and the increasing capital requirements, which makes the process of getting established in farming very difficult? Will "vertical coordination" and corporation farming become the dominant form of agriculture in order to facilitate capital acquisition, resulting in loss of the family farm? The evidence on this point is not clear. However, it would appear the family farm is in little danger in the immediate future if a broad definition of family farm is used.

Despite an over-all decline in the number of farms in the U.S., the proportion of family farms (farms using less than 1.5 man-years of hired labor) is larger now than 10 years ago, and family farms produce 75 per cent of the total agricultural output compared with 67 per cent 10 years ago. However, family farms are larger than they were 10 years ago. Corn Belt farms, though becoming more specialized, still have some combination of crop and livestock enterprises for effective year-round use of family labor and resources. And with livestock enterprises, especially, the "eye of the master" is important.

As pointed out above, traditional credit sources realize that increasing capital is required and are largely meeting the needs. Also, the relatively low returns to capital invested in commercial farms may be an explanation of the lack of real interest in corporate farming and thus the lack of movement of capital from outside agriculture into the operation of individual commercial farms. Thus family farms as a means of control of the resources for farming appears to be rather durable, barring major changes in the structure of farming due to scientific developments or economic forces. The family farms of the future will be larger and will be fewer, but they will remain a dominant force in Corn Belt farming.

The Impact on the Farmer

The commercial family farmer plays many roles as a member of society. He is not only the manager of a large and complex firm. He is often a father, a husband, a church member, a member of civic and business organizations, a voter, etc. What are the tensions that face him because of his role as manager of a large and complex business? How do these tensions affect him in his other roles? How do the tensions affect the effort of the church to minister to him as a "whole man"?

Nowhere are the firm and the household so closely related as they are in farming. This has enabled the farmer to have close ties with his family, but also involves the family in the problems of the farm business. This interrelation leads to both problems and opportunities. For example, on a farm, children can be raised in an environment largely controlled by the family where the values of the parents can be imparted with relatively little outside influence. However, the mental and physical demands of farming must also be shared by the farm family.

The reduction in net income which has occurred for many commercial farmers puts numerous strains on them. The reduction means that less funds are available for investment and/or family living expenses. It also means less opportunity for the amenities of life, the education of the family, vacations, etc. Where the farmer has borrowed large amounts of capital, the problems of repayment may cause tension, especially in the event of unforeseen disaster, such as a drought, sudden drop in prices, or death of valuable livestock.

There is constant pressure on the farmer for increased production. This means the farmer must be alert and aware of new production technology. It also means that he has to obtain the new capital to put much of the new technology to use. He may have to make repayment with lower returns than in previous years. Today's farmers are going to more meetings and spending more time off the farm acquiring information on new technology and thus are away from their families more than previously. The specialization of production also leads to demands on the farmer's time. The farmer on a multiple-farrowing program with 50 sows farrowing during corn harvest may learn to do without sleep for a few days.

An additional concern for the farmer is the future of his children. Will they be able to follow in his footsteps? I imagine most farmers feel their business is a desirable one, and would like to see their children follow in their footsteps. Opportunity for teaching their children farming skills is great because of the interdependence of the household and the firm. But the problem of getting established in farming and making an adequate living forces many farmers to advise their sons to take up an occupation different from their own. On the other hand, those sons who can take up their father's occupation must be well trained in the science and business of agriculture. How to decide if the son should or should not farm and how to provide for his training is a major source of tension. The farmer has lost a great deal of his independence. He does not shape his own destiny as much as in the past. With an increasing amount of his supplies bought off-farm, he has to depend much more upon the suppliers of these materials for the success of his operation. With specialized production, he is also more dependent upon the buyers of his product than before. The actions and decisions of government, local, state, and federal, greatly influence his success. Loss of independence is especially great where large amounts of borrowed capital are used.

Table 2. Average Net Income of Farm Operator Families by Major Economic Classes, United States, 1959

Economic class of farm	Number of farms 1959		Per cent of sales of farm products	Net cash farm income[4]	Average net income of farm operator families		
	Total	Per cent of total			Off-farm income	Total cash income	Total income[5]
Commercial: Farms with sales:							
$10,000 and over	795	21.5	71.9	$6,636	$1,978	$8,614	$9,960
$5,000 to $9,999	654	17.6	15.4	2,165	1,567	3,732	5,018
$2,500 to $4,999	618	16.7	7.4	1,288	2,077	3,365	4,572
$50 to $2,499	349	9.4	1.5	438	525	963	1,476
Other farms:							
Part-time[6]	888	23.9	2.7	176	4,283	4,459	4,890
Part-retirement[7]	404	10.9	1.1	116	1,846	1,962	2,363
All farms	3,708	100.0	100.0	$2,115	$2,247	$4,362	$5,275

Table 3. Farms by Tenure of Operator, 1950, 1954 and 1959

	Illinois			Iowa			Indiana		
	1959	1954	1950	1959	1954	1950	1959	1954	1950
All farm operators	154,652	175,705	195,268	174,685	193,009	203,159	128,193	153,697	166,627
Full owners	63,646	75,640	87,234	79,677	87,984	94,833	75,796	94,188	105,365
Part owners	38,815	38,270	39,771	33,546	30,581	30,229	33,251	30,829	28,615
Managers	451	525	793	391	456	561	379	425	539
All tenants	51,740	61,270	67,470	61,071	73,988	77,536	21,717	28,255	32,108
Proportion of tenancy	33.5	34.9	34.6	35.0	38.3	38.2	16.9	18.3	19.3

Source. 1959 Census of Agriculture.

All of these tensions have developed in addition to the usual tensions caused by the uncertainty of weather and prices which have faced farmers throughout time. As we well know, the individual farmer has little control over weather and prices and can be ruined by drought or a sudden drop in market values.

The church has a challenging role to play in the future. It will not be easy to fulfill this role. As a person whose life was profoundly influenced by a church, I share your hopes and fears for the future.

Table 4. Number of Farms, by Specified Value Groups, United States, 1949, 1954, and 1959

Value group	Number of farms		
	1949	1954	1959
	Thousands	Thousands	Thousands
Number of farms, total	5,382	4,782	3,708
$10,000 and over	484	583	795
5,000-$10,000	721	707	654
2,500- 5,000	882	811	618
Under 2,500	3,295	2,681	1,641

FOOTNOTES

[1]Bogue and Beale, *Economic Areas of the United States,* Free Press, Glencoe, Illinois, 1961.

[2]See: "Resource Requirements on Farms for Specific Operator Incomes," Agricultural Economic Report No. 5, ERS, USDA, February 1962. The price and cost rates used in the study were assumed to reflect prices under competitive conditions, i.e., no price support or production control programs.

[3]For more detailed discussion see: North Central Regional Extension Publication No. 8, "Getting Started and Established in Farming," June 1960, and North Central Regional Publication No. 102, "Opportunities for Beginning Farmers," May 1960.

[4]Cash receipts from farm marketings plus Government payments less production expenses.

[5]This includes nonmoney income from farm food and housing.

[6]Value of sales less than $2,500, operator under 65 years of age and either worked off farm 100 days or more or income of family from nonfarm sources greater than value of products sold.

[7]Value of sales less than $2,500, operator 65 years or older.

4.

LABOR AND INDUSTRIAL DEVELOPMENT

The future role of labor in mid-America will depend upon the characteristics of industrial development in the broadest sense of that word, including all fields of gainful employment without exception: Agriculture, manufacturing, construction, trade, finance, professional and personal services (which incidentally, include the churches and private schools), utilities, transportation, and government (which includes public-supported schools).

Our attention is focused upon the people who make up the communities of mid-America in their role as workers. My comments are, therefore, directed primarily at the development of industries and occupations, and, because of the special character of this development, the educational and training requirements which must be a major concern today.

We know mid-America as an area of lush foliage, rich agricultural lands, thriving cities. The total picture, however, is much more complex. Something of the social and economic problem which exists, in spite of the fertility, productivity, and wealth of this vast region, is indicated by the very slow growth of the region's total population during the past several decades and the actual decline of the rural population over the same period.

For the purpose of considering recent economic developments and trends, it will be helpful to consider the group of seven whole states identified as the West North Central States. These seven states, Iowa, Missouri, Kansas, Nebraska, North and South Dakota, and Minnesota, include most of the area described as the "North Center (Corn Belt) Region." For these West North Central States, much detailed information is available regarding population, industry, and occupational employment trends.

I would like to describe recent population trends in the West North Central States in some detail because they reflect underlying economic developments, and also because people are our prime interest. The growth and the decline of the communities in which people live is a matter of major concern.

We need to investigate the economic factors relating the rapid decline in rural population, and the corresponding growth of urban population. Further, we need to know the significance of these factors, not only to the adult work force which exists, but also to the young people, now in school, preparing themselves for participation in the work force and the community.

The seven West North Central States had a total population in 1960 of 15,394,000 persons, almost 9 per cent of the national total of 179,323,000.

I think we are all familiar with the fact that during the past two decades the rate of growth of population in the West North Central States has been much less than the national growth rate. In the decade, 1950 to 1960, for example, the national population grew by 18.5 per cent, while the population of the West North Central States grew only 9.5 per cent, approximately half as rapidly as the national average.

This small population growth was much less rapid than that which would have occurred on the basis of the natural increase resulting from births and deaths alone. There was, in fact, a net outward migration from the entire area of 820,000 persons, every one of the seven states of the region participating in this process.

Before taking too gloomy a view of that comparison, however, one should note also that the rate of increase of the urban population of the West North Central States, approximately 24 per cent, was near the rate of increase of the urban population nationally, approximately 29 per cent.

The rural population of the West North Central States declined by 6 per cent over the decade, continuing a decline which has persisted for forty years. Nationally, the rural population also declined, but by less than 1 per cent.

The sharp decline in rural population had such a pronounced effect in retarding the growth of the total population of the West North Central States because the rural population is such a large proportion of the total, 41 per cent in 1960. Nationally, the slowly growing rural population constitutes only 30 per cent of the total. Hence, the West North Central States, with its relatively large but declining rural population, is naturally experiencing a much slower rate of total population growth than is the nation. Moreover, this slower overall growth is occurring in spite of the fact that urban places of almost all size groups are increasing more rapidly in the West North Central States.

Thus: During the past decade, the national population living in cities of 50,000 population or more increased 22 per cent. In the West North Central States, population in cities of this size, 50,000 or more, increased 30 per cent. In places of 2,500 to 10,000, the national population increased 18 per cent. In the West North Central States, total population in places of this size, 2,500 to 10,000, increased 25 per cent. Only in the size group, 10,000 to 50,000 population, was the national rate of population growth 57 per cent, greater than that in the West North Central States, 40 per cent.

The main fact to be observed, however, is that the urban population of the West North Central States has increased during the past decade very nearly as rapidly as the national increase of urban population, and urban places of all sizes have participated actively in this growth. The population of cities over 10,000 has increased more rapidly than that of cities below 10,000; but in the West North Central States the total population in these smaller urban places of less than 10,000 population, increased at a much more rapid rate than the total population.

The story of the rural population is quite another matter. In the West North Central States the rural population has declined steadily ever since 1920. The rural population living in communities of 1,000 to 2,500 population actually increased slightly, about 3 per cent, during the past decade, while the total population living in smaller communities and on farms declined by approximately 7 per cent.

The next questions quite clearly are: What economic developments affecting the rural population are causing the long-run decline in this segment of the total population; and what economic developments in urban areas permit absorption of the rapidly growing urban population? And finally, what are the occupational and educational implications of these developments?

The persisting slow increase in the rural population nationally, and the steady decline of the rural population of the West North Central Region is, of course, a reflection of the absolute decline in employment in agriculture.

Nationally, it appears that the high point in farm employment occurred between 1910 and 1917, when approximately 13.5 million workers were employed in agriculture either as hired workers or farm family workers. The decline has been steady since then, but most rapid in recent years, especially since World War II. During the fourteen-year period, 1947 to 1961, farm employment declined nationally from 10.4 to 7.1 million, a decline of approximately 230,000 agricultural workers per year.

In the West North Central States, the change has been similar. Thus, in the West North Central States, the average number of workers employed on farms in 1950, the earliest date for which the regional data are available, was 1,779,000. By 1961, this had declined to 1,307,000, a decline of approximately 472,000, or more than 25 per cent, in eleven years. The rate of decline in agricultural employment during this period was comparably large within the West North Central States and the United States as a whole.

The rapid decline in agricultural employment does not mean that agriculture itself is a declining industry. As a producer of foodstuffs and industrial raw materials, the output of agriculture has increased steadily and very substantially. The annual volume of farm production, in physical terms, has increased by more than one-third during the same period that agricultural employment was declining so rapidly.

At this point, there is one major inference to be recognized, namely, that agriculture, one of the great divisions of industry in the economy, is certainly a declining source of employment opportunities. The industry itself is not declining. In terms of production, it has expanded rapidly, probably too rapidly and for too long. But certainly, the number of job opportunities in agriculture has declined, and under the impact of the continuing advance of technology applied to agriculture, will continue to decline.

Though fewer in number, a larger proportion of the job opportunities which continue to exist in agriculture will require knowledge of the technical aspects of agriculture, of mechanics, and of business. It was probably true of our fathers that, if they were fortunate enough to grow up on a farm, they could become effective self-made farmers. But the successful farmer of today is an educated and technically trained professional. Moreover, his hired man is, most probably, also a skilled worker with at least the technical knowledge and sense of responsibility to operate valuable and complicated machinery successfully.

In other words, over the past several decades, agricultural employment opportunities have become greatly reduced in number, but far more demanding of scientific, technical, and business abilities, with all of the educational requirements which this implies.

Now let us turn our attention to the other industry divisions, the nonagricultural industries. These, in the approximate order of their employment in the West North Central States are: Manufacturing; trade (both wholesale and retail); government; services (professional, business and personal); transportation and public utilities; construction; finance, insurance and real estate; and mining. We find that total nonagricultural employment in the West North Central States increased at exactly the same rate as the national increase, 23 per cent, over the fourteen-year period, 1947 to 1961.

Among the various industry divisions, in the West North Central States, some increased relatively more rapidly, others less so. Manufacturing, for example, in the West North Central States, increased 13 per cent in employment during this period, almost three times as rapidly as the national rate of 4.6 per cent. Trade, on the other hand, equally as important as manufacturing in terms of employment, increased 17 per cent in the West North Central States, but 27 per cent nationally.

Besides manufacturing, the other nonagricultural industry divisions in which West North Central States employment increased more rapidly than the national rate, were construction (up 46 per cent, as compared with a national increase of 39 per cent), and mining, including quarrying and petroleum extraction (up 2 per cent, while employment nationally declined 30 per cent).

Besides trade, which I have already mentioned, the only division of industry which increased substantially less rapidly in the West North Central States than nationally, was government, federal, state, and local. The increase here was 43 per cent, as compared with a national increase of 61 per cent.

In the other industries, services of a professional business, or personal nature (up 44 per cent), and finance, insurance and real estate (up 54 per cent), the increases in employment in the West North Central States were within a few percentage points of the national rates of increase. Transportation and public utility employment declined both nationally and in the West North Central States.

These various figures point to one overall and important fact that non-agricultural employment as a whole in the West North Central States has kept up with the national rate of increase. And one of the most important of the non-agricultural industry divisions, manufacturing, has, during the past fourteen years, increased at a rate much more rapid than the national rate.

For the West North Central States, however, a growth in nonagricultural employment as rapidly as the national rate of increase, while encouraging, is, from many points of view, not enough.

Since agriculture, the single most important division of industry in the West North Central States, is declining so rapidly in employment, it would require a substantially more rapid increase in employment in the other industry divisions than has occurred, to absorb the natural increase in the labor force as well as those workers displaced from agriculture. Although growth of nonagricultural industry has been as rapid in this region as nationally, it has not been rapid enough to accomplish this double objective. Hence, the net emigration from the West North Central States which I referred to earlier, approximately 820,000 during the decade of the 1950's.

For these reasons, much attention has been given to the problem of promoting industrial growth in these states. A general discussion of these efforts would go far beyond the scope of my efforts. However, one aspect of the promotion of nonagricultural industrial growth which I do wish to emphasize is the emerging occupational characteristics of this developing industry and the educational and industrial training requirements which these imply.

The Department of Labor has made intensive studies both of industrial and occupational trends. The industrial trends of the future, we expect, will be much like the postwar development, although there will be regional differences. The most rapid increases in the future will be in construction; finance, insurance and real estate; trade; services; and government. Indeed, in this region, all of these, except trade, increased more than 40 per cent and up to as high as 54 per cent since World War II, and further increase conforming approximately to the national rate, or exceeding it, seems very probable.

Nationally, it is anticipated that manufacturing will increase in employment only about as rapidly as the increase in total labor force. However, as I have already mentioned, during the past fourteen years, manufacturing employment in the West North Central States increased about three times as rapidly as the national rate. Whether this region will continue to expand its manufacturing employment so much more rapidly than the nation, remains to be seen. The prognosis, I would say, is good; but I'm not sure that it is quite that good.

The occupational characteristics of the employed population are also changing in dramatic ways. This is occurring partially as a result of the different rates of growth of different industries, and also as a result of the changing technology within virtually all branches of industry.

Several of the occupational developments follow naturally from the industrial developments, particularly the long continued decline in the number of workers in agricultural occupations, as farmers or farm laborers. Studies made by the Department of Labor indicate that the number of workers employed in agricultural occupations will continue to decline during the present decade at a rate comparable with the recent past. Nationally, the estimate is a 17 per cent decline in the number of farmers and farm workers.

The increases will come in the three other major groups of occupations: The "white collar" occupations (professional, technical, managerial, administrative, clerical, and sales occupations); the "blue collar" or manual occupations, other than farm occupations; and the service occupations.

All of these are increasing, but for many years the white collar occupations have increased most rapidly. In fact, since 1955, the total number of workers engaged in the white collar occupations has exceeded the number engaged in manual occupations; and the white collar group has grown more rapidly ever since.

Within these various categories, we find that the single occupational group which had by far the most rapid rate of increase during the past decade, and is expected to grow most rapidly during the present decade, are the professional and technical occupations. The number of workers engaged in these occupations grew by 54 per cent during the 1950's, and is expected to increase by more than 40 per cent during this decade. These workers include the scientists, engineers, teachers, clergymen, doctors, registered nurses, technicians in business, industry, and other professions, and the arts, approximately eight million employed persons in all in 1960. The occupations of this group, representing the most rapidly growing group of vocational opportunities, have one aspect in common: They all require extensive education and training.

Several of the other groups of occupations, which grew rapidly during the 1950's, and which we anticipate will continue to grow much more rapidly than the total labor force in the future, likewise have higher than average educational requirements. These include the managerial, administrative, and clerical occupations.

Among the manual occupations, only the skilled workers, the craftsmen, foremen, and kindred workers are expected to increase in numbers as rapidly as the total labor force. The number of semi-skilled workers will increase, but less rapidly than the total labor force. Moreover, and this is a fact which should be registered indelibly in our minds, the number of unskilled laborers in nonagricultural industries, which declined approximately eight per cent in the 1950's, will certainly not experience any increase in the 1960's.

The decade in which we are living has many facets, each of which calls for some type of human response. Among these facets are the emerging industrial and occupational characteristics of the economy. These characteristics, both of the nation and of the West North Central States, point certain responsibilities which we have to the young people who are growing up under our influence or guidance.

We can, and I think we must, help them to understand the characteristics of this dynamically growing economy, the kinds of demands it will make upon those who will participate fruitfully in it and the growing and abundant opportunities which it provides.

5.

THE CHANGING
AMERICAN FAMILY

Wherever man is, whatever are the circumstances of his existence, we find the family. While the family is universally found, it is nevertheless true that there is a certain society-to-society variation with regard to the kind of family that is present and the threats, promises, and challenges with which the family is faced. The corollary to this, of course, is that as a society changes over time we should expect to discover changes in its family institution.

My purpose is to examine some of the significant changes in the American family that have recently taken place or are now occurring. My aim is to provide sociological insights about the nature of our family and family living that will be of some utility to the church. At times, however, I will want to go beyond my role as an analytic sociologist and attempt to relate what I think we have discovered about the modern family to the concern of the church.

Before looking at specific changes in the American family, let us talk more generally of social change and its effects. It is a sociological principle that all societies, and all institutions within them, are continually changing. There is no such thing, therefore, as a family institution that is static and never-changing. At the same time, there is considerable variation from society to society and from time to time with regard to *rate* of change in the family. In some eras and in some

47

places, change in the family may be barely perceptible; indeed, a given generation may not even be aware that it is not replicating the system of family values, the roles of family members, the courtship and marriage patterns, the childrearing practices, and other aspects of the family in the generation that preceded it. In other times and in different societies, family change may be rapid, dramatic, and all-encompassing. If we take a long view of human societies over time and a wide view that encompasses all of the societies scattered about the world, it seems quite likely that it is a highly unique experience to live at a time of rapid, far-sweeping social change. Most generations, in other words, have lived out their lives in a period when the family in their society was changing but gradually.

As undoubtedly has been anticipated, we are now living in one of the unique periods of human history characterized by sudden, far-reaching social change. It is at once expected and understandable that there be a certain amount of discomfiture associated with change. At times of rapid change, a given generation will find that habit and tradition are not completely acceptable guides to action, accustomed patterns of behavior are replaced by nuances, and the familiar is superceded by the unfamiliar. Adding to this discomfort, and, indeed, partly responsible for producing it, are the attitudes toward the past that are commonly held, particularly with regard to such an emotionally-charged aspect of life as the family. When we look back at the family of our childhood or, for that matter, at the family in the early days of American society, there is a tendency for our vision to become both blurred and selective. We tend to remember that which was good and pleasant and if we are forced by less kind facilities of the mind to admit to harsher realities, we can at least see them, in retrospect, as "character building."

While not denying that there was good in the family of yesteryear, let us admit that, by almost anyone's definition, there was also bad. One example of what I would label a bad feature of the family of the past can be found in the cold statistics on infant mortality rates. Probably only few today can imagine the sorrows of parenthood when the role of parent all too frequently included burying a little child. The tendency to forget things like this and to remember the pleasant in the past is really fortunate in many respects, but it can hamper our adjustment to the present. Let us, then, simply admit to this tendency to glorify the family of the past and try to avoid it as we turn to the modern version of the American family.

Changing Family Size

One of the changes in the American family which is easy to observe and verify is that of family size. Over a longer period of a hundred years or more, it is true that the proportion of families with six or more children has definitely decreased. It is also true that in the short run of about twenty years there has been a swing away from the one and two child family and an increase in the moderate-size three or four child family. What is more, the childless marriage, having reached a high of about twenty per cent of all marriages, is now down to about ten per cent. This is close to the rate in 1890 when about eight per cent of all married women of completed fertility had never borne a child.

In a heterogeneous society, with its many groups and many differences, it would be expected that all segments of society do not enter into the prevailing trends equally. With respect to the reproductive function of the family, it has been customary to note an inverse relationship between the number of children and both family income and educational level of the parents. While there was a narrowing of this differential for a short time after World War II, there is at present no indication of continued change. The traditional relationship between socio-economic status and family size thus continues to prevail; the wealthier, better-educated, higher occupational groups have fewer children than those with less money, less education, and lower occupational prestige.

It is common to attribute the differential fertility rate by socio-economic status to the unequal spread of contraceptive knowledge in our society; that is, it is often contended that the poorer and less educated groups do not know about, or do not know how to use effectively, the various means for controlling conception. To some extent this may be true, but perhaps it is a misleading oversimplification of the matter. For one thing, this view ignores human motivation in that it fails to ask why people want to limit the size of their families. I am suggesting, then, that we at least entertain the view that lower class couples could, if they wished, control the size of their families but that they simply do not think and feel about family limitation as do middle class couples. Put differently, they have different family values and they have a different definition of what constitutes a good or proper family size.

Very often a pastor finds that in his congregation are people from various walks of life and of different educational levels. He is, of course, the pastor of them all. Typically, the pastor is recruited from and lives in the broad middle class of our society. Perhaps our example of competing values regarding family size that exist within society will allow us to phrase a much broader question: "Can the typical pastor in the typical community really understand the competing values that are held by different segments of the community?" Perhaps we should have asked *how* he can learn to understand the divergent values, for somehow he must come to do so if he is to be effective in his work. I am not suggesting that the pastor should *approve* of all the different values and different ways of life that he sees around him, but I am suggesting that he learn to understand what values the different groups within his community hold and that he learn to appreciate the meaning of these values to the people who hold them. Unless the pastor can come to do this, the charge that the major denominations are "middle class religions" will have some basis in fact.

Class differentials in fertility pertain to rural as well as urban families. This is, the better educated, wealthier, farm owner has fewer children than the less educated, poorer, farm laborer. At the same time, rural families taken together traditionally have been larger than urban families. This differential is still true, but it is becoming less so. Over the last twenty years the difference between rural and urban family size has become increasingly smaller. Rural couples are thus becoming "urbanized" with respect to their family size.

Changing Roles of Family Members

The twin forces of industrialization and urbanization have had a profound effect on the roles of family members, or the parts that people are expected to play within and outside the family. We are all aware, of course, of the declining proportion of American males who earn a living solely by farming. In terms of their role in the family, this means that more and more men find their work physically separated from their home. Fewer men are in charge of a family enterprise, and more men daily leave their homes to earn a living.

The same trend toward nonfarming employment of the male which has been affecting the larger society is also having its influence on the small remaining proportion of workers who are farmers. Increasingly, farmers are seeking off-the-farm employment on a seasonal or part-time basis. This is particularly true of the owners or operators of smaller farms and of farm laborers, for one lure of industrial employment seems to be a financial one.

As industrialization snow-balled through the last century, it had a push and pull effect on the woman of the family. Industrialization pushed women out of the home in the sense that the factories and shops began to take over such traditional tasks as the making of clothes, the laundry, part of the preparation of food, and so on. These same shops and factories that pushed women from the home needed workers, and to meet this need they began pulling women through the factory gates. Women, of course, have always worked. What we are witnessing is a radical shift in the place of women's work that involves an increasing number of women and that is occurring over a comparatively short time. As recently as the turn of the century, less than six per cent of the married women were employed outside the home. Today, in vivid contrast, one-third of all married women work outside the home. The proportion of working wives, as might be imagined, varies considerably over the family life cycle. In the early years of marriage, before there are children, about two-thirds of the wives are employed outside the home. This drops considerably to about twenty per cent of those with pre-school children, but goes up again to about forty per cent of the married women whose youngest child is over six years of age.

At the present time, farm wives are less likely to be working outside the home than rural nonfarm wives and they, in turn, are less likely to be employed than urban wives and mothers. However, the *rate of increase* in the proportion of working wives has been greater among rural women than among urban. The push and pull effects of industrialization are having their effects on the farm wife, with the result that more of them are helping to win the bread in the city, rather than baking it at home.

The same broad forces that have produced the change in the role of women in our society have also affected the role of the child. It used to be said that in the country children are counted as "helping hands," but in the city as "hungry mouths." It is certainly true that under urban conditions each child in the family is responsible for a substantial sum of money on the debit side of the family ledger, which seldom is even partially balanced by his economic contributions. But this is becoming more and more true also of the rural child. With larger-scale farming, the increasing use of expensive and complicated farm machinery, the longer years of education of rural youth, and the many off-the-farm activities that beckon to them, farm boys and girls are not contributing to the productive economy of the family as once they did. In still another way, therefore, is the farm family becoming urbanized.

The changes in the roles of farm family members about which we have been talking are having profound effects on family life and on attitudes toward the family generally. So-ciologists use the concept *familism* to describe a number of interrelated and interpenetrating attitudes that, under some conditions, pervade the life of family members. Some of these attitudes are:

1. A pre-eminent identification of all members with the fam-ily group and their feeling of belonging to it.

2. The feeling that individual objectives should be in accord with, and if necessary, subordinate to family objectives.

3. The feeling that each family member has an obligation to rally to the support of any family member who is in trouble or in need.

4. The sense of security that comes to a given member from the reciprocal expectation that in the event of need he will receive emotional support and tangible assistance from other members of his family.

These ways of thinking and feeling about the family should not be considered the inventions of a morally superior age. These attitudes grew out of basic conditions of farming and rural living that once prevailed. Among these we would in-clude the participation of the various family members in a common occupation; all members, each in his own sphere, were working for a common good. What is more, there was genera-tional continuity in the occupation, for farming as a livelihood and a way of life approached a family tradition. The isolation of the farm family meant that the family had to be the most important group for its members, and that family members had to rely chiefly on one another for their various needs.

The conditions that produced the way of thinking and feeling about the family we have called familism no longer prevail for the vast majority of our people who live in cities and towns, and they are all but gone for the remaining minority on the rural farm. The mechanization of farming and the nonfarm employment of family members mean that in the typical farm family the members are *not* engaged in a common occupation. Rural isolation has all but disappeared, so farm family members can and do look for other groups to meet their needs. With the decrease in the number of farmers needed, farming can no longer be a family tradition for many of the youth must leave the farm for good. Thus, the conditions that produced familism are gone or going fast, but the passing of the attitudes themselves is met with reluctance and regret. It is common to speak of the changes with regard to the economic and social functions of the family as "losses" to the family. To be sure, they *are* losses in the sense that families no longer perform these functions, but it is often implied that these changes also constitute a moral loss, and that the self-sufficient family with jobs for all was somehow ethically superior to the emergent farm family.

Putting together the changes in the roles of the various family members, we can see that, in truth, a new family form is emerging. In the past, the man's position in the family carried with it both a great deal of authority and a great deal of responsibility. Now, at least some, and often much, of the responsibility has been eliminated from his role. He is no longer the manager of a family enterprise, allocating jobs to the different family members. Indeed, with the increase in part-time and seasonal industrial employment of farmers, he is not even physically present on the farm as much as once he was. When the male is absent from the home periodically or usually, sheer necessity demands that some decision-making power be delegated to others. More farm wives working means that more men are sharing in a different way than once was true the responsibility for support of the family. Under such conditions, is it not understandable that the authority associated with the position of the man of the family should decline commensurately with the decrease in his responsibility?

There is evidence, then, that a new family form is emerging and is, in fact, already with us. It is still more an urban than a rural phenomenon, but since the conditions that have led to its development in the city are now also found on the farm, it is to be anticipated that the "new family" will be found increasingly on the farm. In this "new family," husband and wife see themselves as partners and co-leaders in a joint enterprise. In the pure type of the new family, rationality prevails in the sense that neither sex itself nor position in the family carry with them inherent meanings of superiority or inferiority. There is a division of labor between the married pair and there may well be a division of the areas in which one or the other has major responsibility for making decisions; but, again in the pure type of the new family, these things are decided on the bases of rationality and efficiency, rather than on the basis of the traditional family pattern. To use a homely example, it would not be assumed that the man, because he is a male and because he is the husband and father, is therefore inherently more capable of making financial decisions than is his wife. The sort of new family we have been describing goes by many names, some of them not very complimentary, but we can give it the simple label of "democratic family."

The objective social scientist, viewing broad social forces that affect *the* family in the abstract does not find it difficult to note a decline in an older family form and the emergence of a new one. But it is a different matter for those who are required to live with the change in their daily lives. The adults of today were not really prepared for the alternatives with which they now find themselves faced. To use a concrete example, if, or when, or how much a farm wife and mother should work outside the home forces upon today's couple a host of decisions which simply did not exist for almost all of their parents. It is little wonder that modern husbands and wives sometimes experience difficulty in working out roles for themselves which are both mutually agreeable and good for the entire family.

The changes in the roles of family members and in the whole form of the family we are witnessing pose some perplexing problems. Put bluntly, which family values should we endorse? I am not suggesting that religion should, like a chameleon, merely take on the characteristics of the time and the place where it happens to find itself. But neither can religion, if it aspires to be an effective life's force, completely ignore major social changes that are taking place. To continue being blunt, let me raise a few questions: "How important in Christianity is the concept of the patriarchal family?" "Is Christianity incompatible with a democratic family?" "Is it theology, or sentimentality, that says, 'a woman's place is in the home'?" May I presume to suggest that the time is at hand for finding the answers to questions such as these?

Changes in Marriage Stability

Among the various family changes that are taking place, it is difficult to imagine many that are more important to pastors than the changes in the stability of American marriages. Divorce, remarriage after divorce, and the effects of divorce on the couple, on the children, and on society clearly are matters with which we need be concerned. But first some "facts."

At today's divorce rate, out of every four marriages performed, one will end in divorce. This represents the highest divorce rate in the civilized world, a record our society has held for over fifty years. While we have backed off from our high rate immediately after World War II, it is nevertheless true that the long-run trend has been toward an ever-higher divorce rate. At the present time, there is no indication of a reversal of this trend.

Space does not permit a discussion of the many deleterious effects of divorce. Let us simply agree that from many, many standpoints our divorce rate is "too high." This does not imply that there is a "normal" rate of marriage instability, but simply that there are an adequate number of good reasons why our divorce rate should be reduced.

It is one thing to admit that our divorce rate is too high, but quite another to do something about lowering it. Amelioration of the problem clearly demands that we have some idea of what is causing it. The cynic contends that the real cause of divorce is marriage; without marriage, there could, of course, be no divorce. The sociologist agrees that marriage causes divorce, but in a quite different sense. That is, we would contend that there are some ways of defining marriage and of describing the goals that one should seek in marriage that practically insure a relatively high divorce rate.

Over the years, as the family has lost its economic, educational, social, and recreational functions, it has become less and less true that the survival and maintenance of an individual require his living in a family. Gradually the psychological and emotional reasons for getting married and having children have come to the fore, as the practical and obligatory reasons have declined. "Marriage is for happiness" constitutes a not too oversimplified statement of the present-day definition of marriage. Furthermore, our society, as compared with many others, seems to value a high degree of personal freedom in mate selection. These two features of our marriage system, that is, the prominent place of happiness in our conception of a good marriage and the preference for a great deal of freedom in mate selection would seem to have a profound effect on marriage instability. If marriage is for happiness and if the individual is free to pursue happiness in this direction should not he also be free to flee from unhappiness? A sizable proportion of Americans seems to be answering the question affirmatively.

What we have been saying, then, is that the marriage system presumably valued in our society practically implies that there will be some divorce. When so much of the impetus for marriage comes from the promise of close, satisfying, interpersonal relations, it places this aspect of marriage in a vulnerable spot. When the all-important happiness is not found, or is not found in sufficient degree, there are few felt imperatives to remain married.

The question that remains is how far anyone can, or should, go in attempting to redefine marriage in our society. This suggests that religious leaders must continue to address themselves to such time-honored questions as, "What, really, is the purpose of marriage?" and "What is a good marriage?" The answers to such questions will not, of course, immediately solve the problem, but they should at least point to the direction in which solutions can be sought.

The Regulation of Sexual Behavior

There has never been discovered a society that was completely indifferent concerning the sexual behavior of its people. All known societies have somehow come to recognize that it would be too great a disruptive risk to allow their members to have sexual relations whenever and with whomever they please. At the same time, all societies likewise have recognized that it is desirable and even necessary to provide for the sexual needs of their mature members. In all societies, the form of sexual behavior that meets with the highest social approval and which is subject to the fewest restrictions is that which occurs between husband and wife. It would seem, then, that the Christian position that sex within marriage is essentially good, while sex outside of marriage is wrong, is not unduly harsh or unrealistic. It establishes more restraints than are found in some places and more, perhaps, than some would like to see, but it also provides for an approved and legitimate outlet for man's sexual needs.

No pastor in our society needs to be told that the Christian ideal of sex is not a literally accepted value for all Americans, and no pastor can remain indifferent to the violations of the sexual code that he knows exist. The problem becomes that of trying to assess as accurately as possible the extent of violations of the traditional Christian sexual code, the probable reasons for such violations, and, ultimately, of choosing some course of action for dealing with the situation.

Accurate statistics on the rate of nonmarital sexual intercourse understandably are difficult to obtain. The Kinsey studies are now somewhat old and whatever their validity for the period described they do not reflect any changes since World War II. There are, however, some inferential sources of knowledge which can give us a general idea of the situation in recent years. For one thing, the illegitimacy rate has been steadily rising. For another, the venereal disease rate also is rising, particularly among teenagers. On a somewhat more impressionistic level, it has been reported that the number of brides who are pregnant at the time of marriage has been increasing. The conclusion seems fairly obvious that sexual relations outside of marriage are occurring more frequently now than in the past.

If the earlier studies on the extent of nonmarital sexual behavior and if the suggestion that the extent is now even greater are reasonably accurate, what, indeed, should be done and who should do it? In answer to the last question, it would seem clear that the pastor has a major role to play. The expression *major role* is used advisedly, for it has been found that a significant deterrent to sexual behavior outside of marriage is the feeling within a person that such behavior is morally wrong. How to produce this feeling, if such be one's goal, is an admittedly difficult problem. But it is one that it would seem cannot be ignored.

Religion, the Family, and Purpose in Life

My remarks here have brought to light some undesirable and uncomfortable features about the American family today. To have ignored them would have been more pleasant, but it also would have been unrealistic. It is no more realistic or objective, of course, to substitute dark glasses for discarded rose-colored ones. To close on a more positive note, let me indicate quite frankly that I believe the American family has the potential for providing a more meaningful and richer life for all of its members. In a sense I am still looking at the gloomy side of things, for I must add that the family is not achieving its potential to the degree that it could.

The family function of helping to provide a purpose to life is an extremely important one, for there seems to be an inner unrest among Americans and an overriding feeling that somehow life is losing its significance. The feeling of a gradual erosion of meaning and purpose from life cannot be measured and tallied, but its presence can be felt. Perhaps some of it is an unwitting by-product of our societal successes, for certainly less and less of our efforts are being devoted to sheer survival. It would not seem difficult, in other words, to find life meaningful when most of one's efforts are expended in providing the necessities of life for himself and his loved ones, but it is understandably more difficult to wrest deep emotional satisfaction from the knowledge that much of one's efforts go to produce nonessential elements of living.

I am not suggesting that it is impossible to find life meaningful and significant in an affluent society, but I am suggesting that it is difficult to do so. More to the point, it seems likely that we are searching for life's meaning in places where it cannot be found. It would seem that religion and the family are ideally suited as twin forces to deal with the emotional void that seems increasingly to be part of life in a mass society in its time of abundance. From religion man should get broad directions concerning why we are here and whither we are going, and in his family life man should find close, intimate and warm associations with those who share convictions and use them as guideposts in their lives. The fact that neither family life nor religion fulfill these expectations for all of the people all of the time does not detract from the potential of either.

An important obligation of the member of any faith, it seems to me, is to help define the "good life." As a sociologist I would contend that everyone is seriously hampered in this task unless he understands the problem as an individual and as a member of a family. It is because I felt that sociology has something to contribute about the problems and prospects of families that I have written. To the extent that meaningful insights have been provided, will the task be a rewarding experience for me.

6.

AN INTENSIVE LOOK AT
THE SMALL TOWN

The American agriculture industry is faced with a gigantic problem of human adjustment. The Committee for Economic Development, a private organization of industrial leaders, has dramatized the magnitude of this problem in agriculture in a recent publication in which they recommend a program to facilitate the migration of a half million workers a year out of farming into other employment.[1]

Let us review briefly the basis for this migration and adjustment as it was stated earlier in an article I wrote in collaboration with George Beal.[2]

"There is a hard core of consensus among agricultural economists that a reallocation of productive resources is needed in American agriculture. Most economists would agree that the technical revolution of the last half century has made possible a recombination of resources with substantially less labor per farm and more capital and land. If incomes comparable to other alternative employment are an accepted social goal for American farmers, then the economic analysis which points to such a reallocation of resources is straightforward and factual . . ."

"These then are the measurable straightforward economic gains from resource adjustment in agriculture: Money incomes, and probably real incomes of people who *remain* in farming will be substantially higher and move in the direction of comparability to nonfarm incomes as substantial adjustment takes place. This will be true whether or not aggregate output is reduced as a result of the adjustment, because of improved balance between the labor supply and capital and land. There is, however, the question of the intangible human satisfactions which contribute to real income that must be examined more closely.

Money income of the people who *leave* farming will also be higher with adjustment. Probably in most of these cases real income will be higher, but it is under these circumstances that the most serious personal and family problems of social adjustment arise. These cases then will need careful scrutiny.

In addition the total output of goods and services in the economy will be higher if underemployed farm resources are reallocated to higher valued uses. Only in this manner can the gains to economic growth from technical progress in agriculture be fully realized."

Evidence developed since that time continues to confirm that conclusion.[3]

This redundance of labor in farming resulting from technical progress is an inevitable consequence of the impact of economic growth on agriculture. It is one of the principal forces promoting socio-economic change in the towns and communities of mid-America.

Yet before we focus on the small town and the problems farm population mobility has posed we should recognize that the impact of economic growth is not confined to rural areas including small towns. Technical progress in industry, including automation, has confronted labor unions with drastic adjustment. Urban redevelopment faces almost every metropolitan area. Important breakthroughs in science made possible by systematic team research and data processing equipment both expand knowledge in geometric proportions and increase the urgency for education in our society. Education and schools are pressed to keep pace.

The Magnitude and the Impact of Agricultural Adjustment on Small Towns

The 1960 Census reveals that adjustment has accelerated. Using Iowa, which is almost in the center of mid-America, as an example—the number of farms in Iowa declined 8 per cent in the 1955-60 period compared to 5 per cent in the previous 5 years and 2 per cent in the 1945-50 period. The number of farms declined in every county in Iowa. They declined over 5 per cent in 96 counties and over 15 per cent in 31 counties. As farm size increased and farms were recombined, farmers were pushed out of agriculture as well as being drawn out by better nonfarm income opportunities.

Population growth in 1950-60 in Iowa—at 5.2 per cent—was lower than in any of the surrounding states but South Dakota where the rate was 4.3 per cent. By comparison population in the United States grew 18 per cent. Within Iowa population growth was very closely related to urban growth. Strictly farm population declined in every county. By counties, total population changed from a decline of 19 per cent in Appanoose County to an increase of 31 per cent in Linn County.

There is some question about the definition of a small town. Towns with population of under 1,000 would almost certainly qualify. Towns of this size were about equally divided between those which declined (46 per cent) and those which grew (54 per cent).

Much more important, towns close to standard metropolitan statistical areas increased sharply. Incorporated towns within a 25-mile radius of a central city had an average population increase of 39 per cent. On the other hand, the small towns farthest from urban places and not closely related to any central city were much more likely to have declined. For example, there is no central city to which any of the towns in Ringgold, Decatur and Wayne counties are related. All the towns in these counties including the county seat towns had a population decline.

Forces within towns as well as on farms tend toward declining population. Not only does farm technology push farm consolidation but modern transportation and modern retailing and other service technologies also push towards larger and fewer farms. Distance has been shrunk.

As one studies the small towns in mid-America which are almost completely dependent for their economic base on farming, the question is, how have they managed to come as near as they have to maintaining a stable population when their customers, the farm population, have declined so fast. The answer seems to be the expansion in the capital purchased off the farms in the form of such things as power, machinery, fuel, fertilizer, feed and feed additives, and herbicides. The expansion in services in this form has sufficiently offset declines in other retail services to maintain population. Even so one has only to drive through small towns in strictly farming areas to see the impact of the decline. Many store buildings are empty and the investment in housing, public buildings, and retail business is being allowed to depreciate. There is almost no evidence of new investment except for an occasional new house.

To appraise the impact of adjustments in agriculture on small towns realistically it is necessary to look both at those small towns in areas dependent on farming where the town population is declining or stable and also look at the towns that are growing rapidly as a result of immigration from farms to take advantage of expanding nonfarm employment opportunities. There are a number of fairly definite generalizations that can be made about each extreme though the difference between them tends to be a continuum from the sharply declining towns to the small central city suburbs.

Declining towns are characterized by the following trends: Population in the town is either declining or stable with a sharply declining farm population surrounding the town. Population is also aging in the community and especially in the town as young people leave for expanding job areas. With the aging population, the businesses which continue tend not to adopt modern technology or reinvest. They tend to live up the sunk investment as long as possible.

Health services in the town decline as doctors age and retire but modern health services are usually readily accessible within reasonable driving distance.

Local town government is characteristically in the hands of older businessmen whose businesses are declining and who must be very conservative to survive in their business. Even so taxes per capita tend to rise if the population declines. For a detailed study of town government *Small Town in the Mass Society*[4] is excellent, if somewhat disturbing, reading.

Schools are not filled to capacity and buildings are becoming obsolete. One reorganization may be followed within a few years by pressure for a more comprehensive reorganization. School boards tend to be older, conservative people reluctant to face modern demands for education. Both conflicting values about education and reorganization are potential sources of community conflict. Declining communities tend to offer educational opportunities inferior to urban areas.

Churches suffer from the same kinds of problems schools do. Buildings are old and only partly used because of declining population. But reorganization tends to be resisted to the death. (To the death of the church and the spiritual death of individuals—especially young people in the community.) Characteristically the attendance and budget declines and the congregation is held together as long as possible by part-time or lay ministers. The writer attended one such church while camping one weekend at a southern Iowa state park. The church was served by a minister shared with two other churches. There were seven local and ten visiting adults in attendance at the morning worship service. While this town and surrounding farming area had lost half its population, the remaining people were almost totally unchurched.

In the most sharply declining towns a large percentage of the young people eventually seek employment outside the community. Business and job opportunities in town are very limited. A very small percentage may have opportunity to start farming in the community. In a simple study in one such county only about 50 young people are now farming who had started in the last five years.

In the rapidly growing areas the trends are in sharp contrast to declining areas: Population is growing both from natural increase and by in-migration and since in-migrants are typically young, there are more young people of child-bearing age, more children, and fewer old people. In rapidly growing suburban towns, since supporting services tend to lag behind expanding jobs and housing, and since many such services are provided by the nearby central city, it is possible to plan for providing the limited needed services with businesses of adequate size and modern business technology.

It is also possible, however, that in small towns retail businesses may have just enough increased business to delay reconsolidation and perpetuate small relatively inefficient businesses.

Town governments will be confronted with the repeated necessity to expand public facilities such as streets, sewers, sanitation, and fire protection. Taxes will rise but since family incomes usually are rising too it may be easier to pay the taxes.

Schools will tend to be overcrowded. School boards will be confronted with the continual necessity for building programs. Since rural in-migrants may have suffered the handicap of inferior education they may tend to be more alert to the needs for good teachers and curriculum for their children. Churches, too, will be faced with building programs. Also they face the challenge of seeking out and integrating in-migrants, for they all face adjustment problems in the new community.

These generalizations are supported by casual observation but they have also been confirmed by several studies at Iowa State University.

A Framework for Planning

If the foregoing discussion, especially of the declining small town, may sound depressing it does point up the fact that planning to take any kind of social action must start from a realistic confrontation of facts. Much discussion and some action has failed to meet this first elementary step.

The situation is far from hopeless. Adjustments are possible which can raise *per capita* incomes and improve the services of schools and churches to meet both the needs of the young people who are leaving and the older people who stay in declining small towns. These possible social and institutional adjustments are less obvious in the declining communities but adjustments must be made in both types of community if these needs are to be satisfied.

The first step in realism is that whether we as individuals value economic growth in material goods and services or not, our whole social and economic system is keyed to growth. We are not likely to stop either the growth or the adjustment in agriculture that stems from it.

Given a continued growth in the economy it still will not be possible for every mid-American small town to expand its economic base by industrial expansion and hold its natural population increase.

Given economic growth at a sufficient pace to provide job opportunities, as the labor force and technology in the United States expand, adjustment will still be required for per capita real incomes to rise (improved quantity and quality of goods and services including those which churches furnish) in both declining communities and growing communities.

The adjustments will require that some people move to better job opportunities. It will require reorganization of business, schools, churches, and perhaps even county government into larger units. Modern technology makes it possible and requires it if we are to realize our opportunities.

This does not mean, however, that old people should have to move or even seriously disrupt comfortable ways of living. For retired or semi-retired people, Social Security combined with whatever small income they have, usually provides this minimum stability and comfort at the least cost right where they now live with the best opportunity to be as productive as they want to be.

Just as businesses and institutions must be bigger to take advantage of modern technology, the best unit for rational development planning is usually larger than a single small town. Modern transportation makes it possible to cover 50 miles in an hour. Development planning must recognize this. The term central city has been mentioned frequently in this essay. It is symbolic of a planning model developed by Karl Fox.[5]

Conceive of a regional system for development planning composed of open country farms, small towns, county seat type towns, and a central city. The area imports and exports goods and services from and to the rest of the economy. But consumer needs are met at one of these levels within the area. Housing, elementary school, church, gas for the car, and convenience groceries, etc., may be secured in the small town. But this town is related to a larger town for supermarket groceries, the high school, some clothing and furniture, etc. Medical services may be purchased in the larger town or at a clinic or hospital in the central city. Wholesale services, major cultural and theater services, data processing services, manufacturing employment, etc., may only be available at the central city. The system is inter-related and for consumer goods is part of a complete total. Such an area makes development planning more complex, but also widens the range of possibilities appreciably.

Planning can be done within a small town or in a single church within a small town but the restraining variables that must be taken as given and not subject to change, narrow the range of choices as the unit gets smaller.

Implications to Churches

A review of sociological literature, especially with reference to churches in small towns, is depressing. This frustration is especially well-expressed in Peter L. Berger's *The Noise of Solemn Assemblies.*[6] His charge from a sociologist's viewpoint, that the church is not so much a relevant force itself acting on individuals and society as it is an institution giving sanction to the values of American society is not new, but his positive Christian witness as a sociologist to the church is.

How can the church, in Peter Berger's terms, "disestablish" itself from passively supporting the cultural values of the small towns and become a positive force? How can it spiritually equip the young people who leave the community for the life before them in a disturbing urban environment? How can it meet the challenge of some old people in small towns which Berger describes as follows: ". . . There are some Christians whose one vocation remains to suffer and to face death in faith. It is certainly no minor accomplishment if a local congregation provides the communal support for such a vocation."

These questions can be made more specific if applied to the distinctly different problems posed by two Iowa communities, Ackley and Elk Run Heights. Ackley is a rural town growing very slowly. The above questions are appropriate for Ackley. Elk Run Heights is a suburb to Waterloo similar in size to Ackley. The problem it poses for churches is of a different kind. How can these young families really be reached at all by churches and confronted with the message of the church?

The basic answer to all these questions, of course, must be an answer to Berger's question. There is a need for a deep spiritual awakening, a quickened sense of the mission of the church. Failing this there is no answer.

But given this sense of mission and spiritual destiny, these questions are relevant. Somehow the church leaders in the stable or declining community must face the facts of the situation and make decisions. These facts include: If a community has changed, clinging to a "Little Brown Church in the Vale" will not restore what once was. There is evidence that a minimum size of church is necessary for a program that will attract and challenge people—especially young people and as the size of a church declines toward this minimum, cost per person of providing a given level of program inevitably rises. Given modern transportation and these facts, there is a point where consolidation with one or more other churches in the same denomination becomes the only reasonable alternative. (Cross denominational reorganization is, of course, much more difficult.)

Such reorganization is one more acknowledgment that members are living in a larger community, but even with reorganization there may be need for employing some specialized staff such as a religious education director, jointly by two or more churches. The expanding numbers of elderly people need somehow to be better served by the church. A few experiences with saintly old people demonstrate that this should be the time of life for reward in the Christian witness. To face the future with joy and expectancy in old age is the special prerogative of the Christian. Paul in 2 Timothy 4:6-8 expresses this. The church in small towns full of elderly people has a special opportunity to perform this mission of helping them live this way. It can only do it with great difficulty if it is a dying institution itself.

For the fast-growing suburb-type of small town receiving in-migrants, there can be the appearance of success in a church simply because population is growing rapidly. Some of these in-migrants have church attendance so deeply ingrained in their systems that they seek out the church. Attendance can grow steadily by the addition of these people and yet the church itself may have virtually no genuine outreach to the new in-migrants.

Perhaps to reach these unreached, new ways are needed. Perhaps the self-administered discussion-type of adult education activity might serve such a need. In this activity, originated by the Foreign Policy Association for discussion of foreign policy in depth by lay citizens, discussion materials especially designed to substitute for the talk by the expert are prepared to be read by participants before discussion and then discussed in small neighborhood-type groups. Two ends would be served. Such groups would provide a needed neighborhood fellowship contact. They would also enable laymen effectively to discuss difficult subject matter such as theology, confrontation with the Christian message or Christian ethics, and social action.

Perhaps these few presumptuous suggestions are enough to provoke further discussion.

FOOTNOTES

[1]Committee for Economic Development, "An Adaptive Program for Agriculture" 1962.

[2]George M. Beal and Wallace E. Ogg, "Secondary Adjustments from Adaptations of Agriculture," *Problems and Policies of American Agriculture*, Assembled by Iowa State University Center for Agricultural Adjustment, Iowa State University Press, 1959.

[3]In a Jackson County, Iowa, unpublished study of the impact of employment of farmers in a new factory about 95 per cent of the people interviewed considered themselves better off (real income was higher) as a result of the change. Money income data indicated that about the same proportion experienced improved money incomes.

[4]Arthur J. Vidich and Joseph Bensman, *Small Town in Mass Society*, Anchor Books, Doubleday and Co., Garden City, New York, 1960.

[5]Karl Fox, The Study of Interactions Between Agriculture and the Nonfarm Economy: Local, Regional and National. *Journal of Farm Economics*, Vol. XLIV, No. 1, February, 1962.

[6]Peter L. Berger, *The Noise of Solemn Assemblies*, Doubleday & Company, Inc., Garden City, N. Y., 1961.

7.

RURAL VALUES
AND BELIEFS

Basic Beliefs and Values

Functioning as key guides to questions of what ought and ought not be done for the general farm welfare are three sets of beliefs and values, all of which are deeply rooted in American character, particularly American farmers. These are the "work ethics," the "democratic creed," and the "enterprise creed."

A. *The Work Ethic:* A useful point of departure in developing an understanding of our work ethic is the observation that a dominant striving of men the world over is the drive for an increasingly favorable image of themselves in their own eyes and in the eyes of others. This good is the most spiritual (or nonmaterial) of all treasures. You can't get a photograph of it, neither can you weigh it nor store it in vaults or barns; it has no abode in earth or stone—yet we seek it above all else.

But, while the striving for this treasure is common to all cultures, people differ as the night from day with respect to their beliefs on what ways of living and of making a living are prima facie evidence that one possesses qualities of mind and character which entitle him to the high standing he covets.

Our own culture happens to be one which, in part, had its beginning and reached its greatness through the commitment to work ethic beliefs. Four of these beliefs are especially relevant to our problem.

73

First is the belief that increasing excellence in any freely chosen employment is the proper way of earning the finer self image which each of us seeks. Negatively expressed, this belief is the feeling that one fails in his duty to do the best he can by himself, his family, his community and his country if he chooses the "easy" way at the expense of excellence in any employment of his choice, whether making mousetraps, painting pictures, growing corn, or producing sermons and other nonmaterial goods and services. The spirit of this belief is admirably caught up in a conversation between Hiram Goff, a New England shoemaker, and John Jessig, his minister. To strike up conversation Goff remarked:

"I believe in honest work. Work is the law of nature and the secret of human happiness." His minister replied: "I am glad to see a man who can use the humblest vocation to the glory of God as you are doing." This made the shoemaker's hair stand on end. Said he: "There ain't no such thing in this wide world, pastor, as a humble vocation. Listen, you are a minister by the grace of God . . . I am a shoemaker by the grace of God. You'll carry up to the judgment seat a fair sample of the sermons you preach, and I'll carry up a fair sample of the shoes I've been making. If your sermons are your best, and my shoes are my best, He'll say John and Hiram, you have used your talents about equally well. It's just as necessary for people to have good shoes as it is good sermons."[1]

This belief in superior industry as the proper way of earning superior standing includes a firm confidence in a brighter future for all—a confidence that stems from the 200-year interaction of our work attitudes with a virgin continent of opportunities. However severe the privations and cruelties of the new continent, it would nonetheless turn into marvelous shapes and forms under the touch of patient industry. As men saw the oak in the acorn, so they envisioned farms in swamps and thickets, ports and cities in river bends, and paths of commerce along the wild game trails. In this way there emerged the inspiring vision of a formidable continent transforming into farms and homes and thriving cities in response to initiative and diligent industry.

In this way the ethic of industry generates a peculiar brand of practical idealism which has long distinguished our people. As Santayana observed, the typical American is "an idealist working on matter." This fact accounts for his skittishness toward either visionary idealism or crass materialism. Few things get on his nerves more than the preaching of "ideals" that are without tangible promise of such materialistic outcomes as conquering disease or unlocking the secrets of photosynthesis.

Thus, the relationship between "idealism" and "materialism" is like the sides of a coin. The one is inconceivable without the other, although neither is identical with the other. Accordingly, if one calls the usual American a materialist, he scowls. Call him an idealist, and he wonders if you think he is soft headed. But call him a practical idealist, and he dilates with good feeling. Add that he is a self-made man, and he bursts with pride. His "practical idealism" is thus only another name for his work ethic—his belief that men possess ample means for bringing their present conditions increasingly in line with their dreams or visions through an ever greater mastery of nature, both human and physical.

In addition to generating a deeply confident faith in a brighter future and an intensely practical idealism, the ethic of industry includes important concepts of equity. For the belief that a key responsibility of the individual is to earn ever higher standing through increasingly superior industry obviously includes the reciprocal beliefs that society owes to each individual (a) the opportunity to productive roles in keeping with his capabilities, (b) the right to receive fair payment and recognition in return for his contributions, and (c) the opportunity to develop his productive potential as fully as possible. In line with these deep-seated work ethic beliefs, we strive for a society that offers all men productive roles; and we resent the unfairness of individuals who seek a living and a favorable valuation of themselves but are unwilling to earn these treasures through superior industry.

B. *The democratic creed and the enterprise creed:* As deeply rooted in American life as the work ethic beliefs are the democratic and enterprise creeds. The key components of the democratic creed are the beliefs that all men are of equal dignity and worth and that none, however wise or good, is good or wise enough to have arbitrary power over any other.

Two components of the enterprise creed are especially relevant to our problem: Proprietors deserve exclusive right to prescribe the working rules of their productive units. Therefore, a prime function of government is to prevent anyone, including government itself, from restricting the power of proprietors to run their businesses as they like.

C. *Opposite meanings of freedom:* These two creeds include opposite meanings of freedom. Embodied in the enterprise creed is a negative sense of freedom. To be free is to be left alone, unmolested by collective restraints on the managerial power of proprietors to run production units as they see fit.

Clearly, this meaning of freedom does not derive from the democratic beliefs that all men are of equal dignity and worth and that none, however wise or good, is good or wise enough to have arbitrary power over any other. No mere absence of collective rules follows from these premises. What does follow is that all individuals (or their legal representatives) by nature are entitled to an equal voice in deciding on the common rules which all must observe for the sake of their common welfare. The hallmark of free men is not mere exemption from collective rules but the positive role of each in making his voice heard and his opinion felt in determining what collective restraints they will impose upon themselves for the sake of their mutual welfare.

Thus the positive concept of freedoom inherent in our democratic creed is use of collective action through government or other means to achieve protection or liberation from hazards, including loss of property or jobs, inadequate remuneration, arbitrary hiring and firing, unemployment, and retirement insecurity. Using this concept of freedom, American people have achieved liberation from many oppressive ills.

The work ethic, the democratic creed, and the enterprise creed—these are the deep-seated beliefs and values that have functioned as the chief guides to making decisions since early times in America.

Let us now take a closer look at the connection between our work ethic beliefs and the surge for scientific and technological advance that has unfolded and continues to unfold in our Machine Age. Three illustrations will bring out the connection.

As we all know, a most striking expression of farm technological advance over the last 15 years is the dramatic reorganization of the pre-World War I system of 6 million farms into a continually decreasing number of larger units. Three classes of farm people are involved: those achieving larger units; those leaving agriculture; and those "boxed in" on inadequate farms, unable to move up to larger units or move out of farming.

Evidently the ethic of industry animates all three classes. First, the drive of those who are successfully reorganizing our older system of farms into fewer and larger units is not so much the mere materialistic thirst for money as it is the aversion to being guilty of deeds that deserve low standing. To be sure, the higher incomes achieved through their superior industry do meet their need for material livelihood. But the more basic fact remains that the larger fields and faster moving machines they gather about themselves also meet the more profound spiritual need for evidence that they are the kinds of persons who deserve a far greater measure of respect and esteem of their own as well as that of others, than would be the case if they sat in the shade more and put a higher premium on hunting and fishing. In the absence of this powerful ethical drive, it is questionable if the so-called materialistic income incentives would cause as much as a ripple in the American countryside.

The same reasoning evidently applies to great numbers now leaving their inadequate farms. It is difficult to envision more striking evidence of the extent to which all walks of American life are impregnated with the aspiration for merit through superior industry than this fact: more people than now live on farms have migrated since 1930 in quest of better paying nonfarm employment.

Finally, the same work ethic is evidently the root of a great deal of tragedy and pathos on the part of many thousands who, for one reason or another, are unable to escape their inadequate farms, either through migrating to higher paying nonfarm employment or through reorganizing their holdings into larger units. Strange indeed it would be if they did not see in their scanty acres, weather-beaten buildings and run-down equipment the evidence of failure to fulfill their aspiration for higher standing through proficient industry. In this way, the work ethic generates an anguish of spirit that cannot be assuaged by any amount of income that might be bestowed upon them by beneficent friends or a concerned government. Many may enjoy the pride and self complacency which comes from the feeling that one has met rather well the work ethic test of favorable valuations of his worth, but the sobering fact remains that many are also bruised and broken, perhaps beyond repair, by its strenuous demands. One may or may not hold the ethic of industry to be a noble ethic, but none can deny that it is a hard task master; it contains no balm for sinners.

The dependence of the so-called economic incentives on work ethic beliefs is forcefully brought home by a look at opposite traditionalist beliefs which characterized our Western society until the 1600's, and which still characterize most of the so-called underdeveloped countries. It is commonly recognized in these cultures, that the quest for personal significance is largely guided by the belief that if one is exempt from economic employments it is evidence that he possesses qualities which entitle him to highest standing; and if he works for a living, it is proof that he is so devoid of meritorious capacities that he deserves only the lowest ranks. Thus, work is irksome, not because it is strenuous, but because it is the badge of inferior worth, even servility. Since a favorable image of oneself in one's own eyes and the eyes of others is the most prized of all goods, commitment of mind and conscience to this belief means that one feels duty-bound to limit his expenditure of time and energy in economic employment to the minimum required to support his customary way of life. Rooted in this belief, reason and conscience can offer no explanation, except greed or miserliness, why anyone should forego leisure for the sake of doing more work than is necessary to support his customary need.

Present-day literature abounds with evidence that under the guidance of this traditionalist belief, the so-called incentives of higher wages or profits are relatively ineffective inducers of greater productive effort.[2] For example in the latter part of the 19th century, Weber observed that in East Germany farmers often tried to induce workers to speed up the harvest by raising the piece rate. They usually found, however, that this resulted in less work instead of more:

"The worker reacted to the increase not by increasing but by decreasing the amount of his work. . . . The opportunity of earning more was less attractive than that of working less. He did not ask: How much can I earn in a day if I do as much work as possible? But: How much must I do to earn the wage, 2½ Marks, which I earned before and which takes care of my traditional needs."[3]

The same principle applied to the business classes as well as the working classes. Speaking of early day German textile industry, Weber further observed that:

"The form or organization was in every respect capitalistic: the enterpreneur's activity was of a purely business character, the use of capital, turned over in the business, was indispensable; and finally, the objective aspect of the economic process, the bookkeeping was rational. But it was traditionalistic business, if one considers the spirit which animated the enterpreneur: . . . the traditional manner of regulating the relationships with labor and the essentially traditional circle of customers and the manner of attracting new ones."[4]

There is thus no mystery in the fact that participants in efforts to promote economic development in the so-called "underdeveloped countries" have noted—often with bafflement and dismay—that progress is thwarted by the unresponsiveness of the people they are trying to help. Higher profits or wages do not become effective inducers of productive effort until the powerful quest for personal significance is tied to the belief that increasing proficiency is a proper way of earning high standing.

Our Machine Age is mainly the outgrowth of a deep-seated commitment to this work ethic and not the other way around. On the rural scene, this truth best unfolds from the vantage point of an earlier day when land was so abundant as to be "dirt cheap" while the human factor was scarce as to be extremely dear. In this setting nothing was more obvious than that the desire for earning increasingly favorable valuations of one's personal worth through proficient industry lay in discovering new implements and machines that would increase the amount of land and materials which a man could handle. In response to this belief, American farmers became notorious tinkerers long before the birth of agronomists and agricultural engineers. It is an inspiring experience to read how the most outstanding of these tinkerers such as McCormick, Oliver, and Deering, first conceived and brought forth many of agriculture's implements and machines.[5]

But farm people were the first to recognize that from their own tinkering could never come the technical knowledge that was needed to give vent to their aspiration for a better life through superior industry. They were sure that this new kind of knowledge would have to come to them as a specialized service from a larger social order, which did not then exist. For the kind of knowledge then supplied by the existing order was serviceable, by and large, only to those exempt from manual employments, such as lawyers, artists, and ministers; it was useless to the ordinary farmer seeking a cure for a sick calf or trying to make two blades of grass grow where only one had grown before.

Therefore, in line with the work ethic belief that society owes its members an equal opportunity to the means necessary for developing their productive potential to the fullest extent possible, farm people sought a government that would provide them with specialized knowledge through establishing agricultural research and educational institutions. With the passage of the Morrill Act of 1862, there emerged a government that increasingly undertook responsibility for meeting this need. In the history of the Republic, there is no finer chapter than how the Nation's effort to meet this need began with little more than a sprawling farm on which some experienced farmer instructed young men in the best-known farm practices of his time, and how within the short span of a century this became the modern system of Land Grant Colleges, Experiment Stations, and Extension Services that is today the wonder of the world.

From these and other vast incubators of new farm knowledge there now flows an ever hastening stream of technical innovations on so many fronts and at such rapid rates as to generate farm production capacity faster than domestic population growth, rising per capita incomes, and farm exports are able to generate new market outlets at reasonable prices.

This jarring fact is abundantly illustrated by the experience of the 1950's. Prior to that time, the almost unquestioned presupposition was that a prosperous national economy would take at reasonable prices all the food and fibers farmers could produce, and also provide higher-paying nonfarm employment opportunities for all farm workers not needed in agriculture.

But the 1950's up-ended this presupposition. For this decade witnessed a national economy of unprecedented peacetime high levels of employment and rapid gains in national production. But the farm side of the economy is a very different story. At the close of the Korean War (1952) total farm production and total demand were in balance at 100 per cent parity levels.[6] Throughout the 50's farm production increased on the average of 2.6 per cent per year. This compared with an average gain of only 1.6 per cent in total demand, due to population growth, rising consumer income and exports. This imbalance resulted in an annual rate of surplus production of about 6 to 8 per cent by 1960.[7] Moreover, this imbalance did not arise from the use of more total resources but from technical advances that increased production from approximately the same total resources.[8]

During the 1952-60 period, prices paid by farmers rose by 4 per cent, but the prices they received fell by 18 per cent.[9] Net farm income fell from about 15 billion dollars in 1952 to about 11 billion in 1960.[10] Prior to 1954, the decline resulted in rising costs and price depressing surpluses, as prices were then above parity support levels. From 1954 on, the decline reflected a combination of rising cost, continued surplus production and falling of price support levels.

Thus the lesson of the 50's is clear. For a long time to come, high levels of employment and rapid growth of the national economy may be accompanied by a large excess farm production capacity and price-depressing surpluses.

In this way, the very technical advance long called for by the belief of farm people that increasingly superior industry is the proper way of earning ever higher standing throws into sustained conflict their deep-seated work ethic and enterprise beliefs. Here is the conflict. Farmers tend to want a program that will balance farm production with demand at fair prices. Such a program would help them share equitably with society in the cost-reducing benefits of an increasingly superior industry and technology. But the price for such a program includes collective restraints on farmers to run their businesses as they please.

Thus the farmer's technology puts his deep-seated beliefs and values in jeopardy. At issue is not the question of the democratic freedom of each to have an equal voice in laying down the rules; rather the issue is from which malady does the farmer most want to be liberated. Does he most prize a democratic order that places some restraint on farming as he pleases in order to permit him to receive an equitable share of the benefits of his increasingly superior industry? Or does he want most a democratic order that deprives him of a fair share of rewards, but leaves undisturbed the privilege to farm as he pleases? Either choice is consistent with our democratic creed. The value conflict that is thus generated by our highly productive farm technology and limited markets is strictly a clash between our work ethic desire for equity and our enterprise desire for no constraint on management of business.

Whichever policy they choose, farmers will remain a free people. If they choose to handle their excess productive capacity through democratically established and effective supply-management programs, they will enjoy liberation from economic conditions that preclude them from sharing equitably in the cost-reducing benefits of their industry. If, on the other hand, they choose to take whatever the market offers them for their goods and services, they will enjoy liberation from democratically imposed restraints on their prerogatives to run their businesses as they like.

From which of the maladies do they most seek liberation? This is the hard question. Both liberties are treasures but the cost of one is some sacrifice of the other.

This conflict tends to deprive us of sure knowledge of precisely what is good, what is right, and what is our responsibility. This is precisely the nature of our serious policy (ethical) problem.[11] As individuals and as a country, we are often in situations in which we know what line of action is right because we are not faced with conflicting beliefs and values. In such situations we know what our duty is and our only problem is that of having enough will power to do what we ought to do. But the heart of the issues under consideration here is the clash of deep-seated beliefs and values that have guided us since the formation of the Republic, and even before that.

In these situations, our trouble is not the lack of will to do what we already know is right, but the lack of clear ideas of what action is really right.

We resolve problems like these only as we are able to adjust the relative importance of our competing beliefs and values, and we do this through weighing the desirability of alternative courses of action, carefully forecasting and measuring the results of each alternative. This does not mean that all parties will reach the same decision on what ought to be done. For like justices of the Supreme Court, people often give different weights to the same evidence.

This means that no amount of scientific analysis can ever predetermine uniformly right answers to any given policy question; it can only point out the conditions that will generate conflicts among our traditional beliefs and values, suggest alternatives to our present rules, and forecast their outcome. But, policy conclusions turn on what weights people give to scientific findings and since each individual (or group) is his own unique weighing mechanism, no amount of measurement can ever grind out the answers to a policy question. It can only give us data that are relevant to policy deliberations.

From which of these maladies do we most seek liberation through democratic procedures? This is the real issue. Until we tie down the specific ills from which we most seek liberation, there is scarcely a whiff of wind between the teeth so devoid of meaning as the word freedom. But this fact is brushed aside by the easy confusion of the negative concept of freedom in our enterprise creed with the positive meaning of freedom in our democratic creed.

We are able to generate an almost unbelievable degree of destructive fervor through permitting the negative sense of freedom in our enterprise creed to masquerade as democratic freedom. This confusion of meanings makes our powerful allegiance to democratic beliefs the handmaiden of the enterprise belief that our American way is threatened by collective action in line with our work ethic demands for more equitable rules of living and of making a living. In this fashion, the enterprise concept of negative freedom is continually used in opposing needed social legislation on the ground that it would destroy our democratic way of life.

If there actually be a serious threat to our democratic way of life, it may reside in this confusion of the meaning of freedom in our democratic creed, according to which free men are those who have an equal voice in making the rules which they all must observe for the sake of common welfare, and the quite different meaning of freedom in our enterprise creed according to which free men are those who enjoy absence of collective restraints on individual action. For this confusion chokes the impartial quest for basic facts by generating the mistaken conviction that our fundamental policy alternatives are actually choices between total good and total evil, whereas it is actually between competing goods, each of which has faults as well as merits.

Our course of inquiry leads to three general conclusions that deserve mention. The philosophical aspect and the economic aspect of any serious policy problem is as inseparable as the sides of a coin. Generally speaking we decide on what changes we are willing to make in our traditional rules concerning the economic aspects of life only as we are able to appraise these rules from the standpoint of the changes they will force us to make in the relative weights or importance which traditionally we have given our basic creeds concerning proper ways of earning an ever finer image of ourselves in our own eyes and in the eyes of others.

Therefore, to say that the philosophical aspects of any serious problem are any less or more important than its economic aspects, makes as little sense as to say that one side of a coin is any less or any more important than the other side. Hence, to function most effectively in the resolution of policy problems, it is just as important to become skilled in the knowledge of our beliefs and values as it is to become skilled in the knowledge of economic variables. The more we are able to improve our proficiency in both skills, the more our research and measurement activities will be guided with an eye to vital issues, and the more our policy deliberations will be guided by an understanding of basic facts concerning the relative merits and faults of competing goods instead of abstract doctrines concerning total good and total evil.

FOOTNOTES

[1]Cited by Fredrick Brown Harris, The Evening Star, editorial page, Washington, D.C., October 30, 1955.

[2]The author has developed this theme more fully in "Beliefs, Values, and Economic Development," which appeared in the November 1961 issue of the Journal of Farm Economics.

[3]Weber, Max, "The Protestant Ethic and the Spirit of Capitalism," London, 1930, pp. 59-60.

[4]Weber, p. 67.

[5]See e.g., Bidwell, Percy Wells, and Falconer, John I., "History of Agriculture in Northern United States 1620-1860," pp. 204-216 and 281-305, The Carnegie Institution, Washington, D. C., May 1925.

[6]"Agricultural Prices," U. S. Dept. of Agri., Statistical Reporting Service, Crop Reporting Board, Washington, D. C., June 1961, Table I, p. 5.

[7]Whitmore, John M., and Abel, Martin E., Learn, W. Elmer, and Cochrane, Willard W., "Policies for Expanding Demand for Farm Food Products, Part I History and Potentials," University of Minnesota Agricultural Experiment Stations, St. Paul, Minn., 1958, p. 97.

[8]"Changes in Farm Production and Efficiency," U. S. Dept. of Agri., Statis. Bul. No. 223, Washington, D. C., July, 1961, table 23, p. 47.

[9]Derived from "Agricultural Prices," op. cit., Table 6, p. 6, Table 7, p. 8.

[10]The Farm Income Situation, FIS-183, U. S. Dept. of Agri., ERS, July 1961, Table 3, p. 35.

[11]This logical or intellectual characteristic of serious policy (ethical) problems was first identified by John Dewey in his analysis of the "moral situation." See Dewey, John and Tufts, James H., "Ethics," Henry Holt and Company, New York, 1908, pp. 205-211; and revised edition 1932, pp. 173-176. On this point also see observations of Gunnar Myrdal on the moral nature of any social problem in "An American Dilemma," Harper and Bros., Pub., N. Y. 1944. p. XLvil.

8.

FAITH IN AN AGE OF ABUNDANCE

"I hold that the name Paradise applies to the whole world. . . . In our time God has cursed fruitful lands, caused them to be barren and unfruitful by reason of our sins, for where God gives not His blessing, there grows nothing that is good and profitable, but where He blesses, there all things grow plentifully, and are fruitful."

From *The Table Talk of Martin Luther*[1]

The subject of these pages requires the application of beliefs and values to problems confronting the midwestern farmer and the rural and small town community. The perspective from which it is to look at town and country problems is that of the Lutheran congregation standing in the Lutheran tradition and nurtured by the Lutheran theological understanding of the church and the world outside the church. The subject requires that an opinion be offered about the responsibility of the Lutheran congregation in the situation of rapid rural change, but that a companion emphasis should be upon beliefs and values deriving from our theological tradition which should be helpful as a value and belief structure for the individual Christian clarifying the meaning of life and establishing worthwhile goals toward which to reach when making decisions.

In contemplating this I am led to agree with Luther in his commentary on Genesis 3:19 when he writes that of the work of the farmer, the officer of the state, and the teacher of the Church, the last named is the most difficult.[2]

I. The Lutheran Church and Social Action

The need for a topic as this derives from the fact that traditionally Lutheranism has had an ambiguous reputation, being credited with quietism on the one hand and significant cultural influence on the other. This reputation is confusing and requires comment in order that it be put in perspective.

In his understanding of civil government and even in his concept of the basic structure of society Luther retained medieval views. Particularly in respect to resistance to governments Luther was conservative, as was Calvin. But Luther went further than Calvin and granted the princes a great deal of power in the church. Calvinist churches which were more independent of civil influence and considered themselves to be the conscience of the state have taken up the role of dissent more often than Lutheran groups. There is some justification, then, for the claim that part of our Lutheran tradition was quietistic. Also with particular reference to the modern American situation it should be noted that there is no specific foundation in Luther's teaching on government for popular democracy, nor, in fact, is there in Luther's teaching any appreciation for the high mobility and fluidity found in our contemporary society. On questions of government and society Luther was more of a medievalist than a modern.

When we evaluate the American experience of Lutheranism, we note that Lutheran church bodies until recently have not been active in movements for social change. A number of factors, it appears, hindered the earlier expression of Lutheran church opinion on social problems or Lutheran church participation in reform action. Many of the Lutherans who emigrated from the Old World were strongly influenced by Pietism which was extremely individualistic in its emphasis. Another important factor was the slow adaptation of the immigrant church to the American scene. Typically, the last part of the immigrant culture to be Americanized was the church. Then, too, the prevailing Protestant ethic of the 19th century was an individualistic distortion of the Reformation ethic, and the social ethic which developed in the Social Gospel movement at the end of the 19th century was popularly associated with a liberal theology which was unacceptable to confessional Lutherans.

For these and other reasons Lutheranism in America has not developed a tradition of working through congregations or denominational agencies for improvements in society. Most of the emphasis in Lutheran bodies upon congregational and denominational responsibility in dealing with social problems has arisen within the last few decades. Viewed historically, then, it is not surprising that Lutheran congregations are somewhat slow in identifying with community interests and projects for community improvement. Historical tradition does not yet confirm the congregation or denomination in this role.

Lutheran congregational life, moreover, is more characteristically of the church-type than the sect-type. The Lutheran congregation tends to be much more inclusive in membership than the sect-type congregation and thinks of itself more in terms of administering the means of grace than as an institution called of God to separate the elect from the nonelect. It has not traditionally enforced rigorous holiness standards as criteria for membership, nor has it as a denomination made it a condition of membership to manumit slaves, declare for pacifism, join the temperance movement, or renounce all private property. It has not, in fact, even enforced a tithe. The greater emphasis within the Lutheran church has been upon testing for doctrinal orthodoxy than upon testing for individual commitment to denominationally agreed upon standards of individual or social righteousness.

Since it is the nature of the Lutheran church to be primarily concerned with administering the means of grace allowing God to be the judge of the truly elect, the means by which the Lutheran church can enforce its social position is limited to preaching, teaching programs in its auxiliary movements and to the issuing of social pronouncements.

While it is true that the tradition and character of the Lutheran church contain obstacles to the achievement of effective Lutheran denominational and congregational social influence, these obstacles are neither insurmountable nor do they by any means outweigh the positive contributions of Lutheranism to a truly meaningful Christian social influence. Prime among the positive Lutheran assets are a dynamic, constructive religious understanding of the role of the Christian in building a just and satisfying society and the determined insistence upon the freedom of the Word of God to operate within the church and the larger society. The judgment of life by the Word of God is the critical principle in Lutheran social action and the religious embracing of the world by the Christian in the creative principle in Lutheran social action. First, let us examine the critical principle.

The Critical Principle of Lutheran Social Action

While Luther rejected the idea of the ecclesiastical control of society represented in the Catholic concept of Christendom, he did not repudiate the idea of Christendom. He freed the state from specific ecclesiastical control because he realized that the institutional church itself was subject to corruption and did not represent an infallible source of wisdom for guiding either the spiritual or temporal life. This is evident from his refusal to identify the true Church with any specific institution. What Luther did was to demand that both the church and the state be responsible to an authority which stood above, beyond, behind, and yet within any historical embodiment of church and society.

In this move there was no intention of secularizing the realm of society, for it was not a repudiation of the idea of Christendom but a transfer of ultimate authority in both church and society from a human to a divine source. This was a religious revolt against the assumption of absolute authority by any king or spiritual lord. There was a King of kings and Lord of lords. It was a prophetic call to remind the church and the state of

the supratemporal authority to which they were both responsible. The instrument to effect this acknowledgment of a higher
authority by all human authority was the Word of God and
Luther insisted that of prime importance in Christendom was
the free proclamation of the whole counsel of God to every
segment of society.

This emphasis upon the absolute sovereignty of God and
the correlative idea of the relative truth or goodness of every
temporal embodiment of truth or righteousness is of great importance when evaluating social change. From this perspective
there is nothing historical which can lay claim to being a final
formulation. Every tradition, even that which is hoary with
age, must be subjected to the test of whether or not it represents the will of God in the present. This is as true of Lutheran church traditions as it is of the traditions of society.
Nothing temporal is beyond criticism and the need for change.

Moreover, the Word of God which stands in judgment over
our personal and social histories calls for renewal at ever
higher levels of conformity to the expressed will of God. Justice and human welfare are never final achievements even
from a human perspective but the divine righteousness and
concern which is held before us in the Holy Scripture is of
such an order that there can be no sense of the satisfaction
of requirements in any of our attempts. Coincident with the
proclamation of the sovereignty of God must be a divine dis-
content.

Now it follows from the Lutheran principle that it is the
responsibility of the Church which has been given the Word
of God to witness to the sovereignty of God and also to the
failures of the Church and society to conform to his will. This
function of the ministry of the Word of God is discharged
when the law of God is preached, included in a proclamation,
or addressed to a person or a group in private or public counsel. It follows from this principle that it is the duty of the
minister of the Gospel and of the congregation to speak that
Word of God, which is sharper than any two-edged sword,

in order that it be free to convict its hearers and bring change. It is significant that when the church is truly the church fulfilling its function of proclaiming the Word of God, it also discharges a most valuable social responsibility. By a relevant and proper preaching of the law of God it prepares people—farmers, businessmen, community leaders, teachers, preachers, housewives —all of us—for change.

The Creative Principle of Lutheran Social Action

While Luther's specific views on government and the structure of society were time bound, his theology was dynamic and is as relevant today as in the sixteenth century. As a result, the ethical insights which come from Luther's theology are not inextricably tied to a medieval social perspective. Substantiation for the continuing cultural significance of Lutheran beliefs and values is found in the folk culture of Germany and Scandinavia and from Lutheran communities within the United States. Though many of Luther's specific social views were medieval, Lutheranism, even modern Lutheranism, has not been restricted by this liability to influence on private character alone. Lutheran folk cultures have developed which are spiritually and ethically dependent upon Lutheran faith.

The basis for this influence has been Luther's understanding of how God works with men to build lives and communities. The place to begin this explanation is with faith. Faith for Luther was a living, active thing which by its nature was creative. It represented an open, positive attitude which was willing to venture. Furthermore, faith, for Luther, was necessarily active in love. Faith in Christ meant activity which built up, reconciled, former connections, and granted not only justice but the more personal concern of love. If faith was the creative element, love was the formative principle which gave the creative activity specific character in terms of appropriate customs, laws, and deeds.

It was through faith and in love, Luther held, that the Christian was allowed to participate with God as a co-worker as God provided for man and built community. Far from being foreign to his faith, the Lutheran Christian who understood Luther, held the creation of family customs, work traditions, laws, and community folkways to be part of his privilege of working with God. Here his faith which trusted in the guidance of God was active in the Spirit to build a godly structure. "Unless the Lord build the house, those who labor, labor in vain" (Ps. 127:1).

This understanding of the high calling of the Christian man is the creative principle of Lutheran social action. It achieves a widely dispersed influence since it works through scattered individuals. But behind this activity was no law of automatic harmony or dialectical materialism but the active presence of God as participant in the unfolding drama of history. In all things God was working for good and he called men to work with him.

In summarizing the relation of the Lutheran church to social action, it can be said that while historically the Lutheran church has received a reputation for quietism, much of which is deserved, its theology and ethical dynamics bespeak for it a creative role in social action through the Christian laity. Lutheran social action, furthermore, is best expressed by the denomination and the congregation when it seeks to do well what it is called to do; namely, to proclaim the whole counsel of the Word of God. The church is not called to assume socially coercive measures or to be involved in political power struggles but to proclaim to every segment of society the demands of a sovereign God.

II. The Christian Laity and Christian Vocational Fellowships

The creative social influence of Lutheran faith is centered in the individual Christian as he is active in his calling. According to Emil Brunner, "When Luther drew forth this forgotten truth from beneath the rubbish heap of ecclesiastical ethic—it was an act of significance for the whole of world history, an act of overwhelming importance."[3] What Luther did was to turn the dynamic of Christian discipleship away from specifically ecclesiastical acts into the ordinary channels of life. The Protestant Christian whose fellowship with God was established by an act of grace through Christ was freed from the ecclesiastical system of the accumulation of merit. His dedication to Christ in his ethically active "new being" was to be expressed by living a life of trust in God and loving performance of good works in the God-ordained activities of life which were the various roles of ordinary society. It was there rather than in a monastery that the Christian could truly serve God, because it was in the work of the world that God was actively working for good. By serving men in faith and love the Christian also was serving God. As Brunner has suggested, this redirection of religious zeal has had unending significance in social development.

This understanding of the social role of the Lutheran Christian, however, has been confronted by two basic difficulties within recent times. On the one hand it has suffered from the popularity of a piety which accepts the idea of separate sacred and secular realms. Much modern religion believes that religion has to do only with personality development, family standards, personal habits, and specifically church functions. Religion has been restricted to the private life or to an institutional involvement. This is one of the features of the attenuated Protestant piety which is found in our rural, urban, and suburban churches. In practice the assumptions of secularism prevail in the public roles of numerous privately pious people. There are forces at work in our society which bring into question the assumptions of secularism—forces which are extra-ecclesiastical. But the great need in our churches, in specific reference to this difficulty, is for such forceful preaching and teaching of the clear Word of God that those who claim the name of Christian will acknowledge the sovereignty of God in every sphere of life. This is also necessary so that Christians will see God's activity in the actual work of the world and will venture in faith and love to be his co-workers in their public roles.

A second difficulty preventing the full realization of the social dynamic represented in this Protestant embrace of the world, is the problem of knowing what is the Christian thing to do when the ethical issues get complicated in the actual situation of change. The situation which Luther faced when he wrote about the calling was stable, with wide agreement on the responsibilities involved in the various functions. There was then a cosmos of callings, a well-ordered system of social roles. Furthermore, most relationships were face to face or primary relations as we could call them today. It is understandable that Luther could count on the ethically instructed intuition of the Christian to know what to do.

The Puritans, who took the idea of the calling seriously found the situation in seventeenth century England sufficiently complex to call for case books which gave direction in cases of conscience and set out generalized rules for accomplishing the most good. Such examples of Protestant casuistry were continued into the 18th and 19th centuries and guided our Puritan forefathers in America.

In the twentieth century as the rate of change has accelerated, dramatically bringing great mobility and fluidity to our society as well as increased complexity in our relationships, private ethical intuition and case-book casuistry have proven to be insufficient guides to many ethical decisions. There has been an obvious need for the accumulation and dissemination of social intelligence and ethical insight. Recognizing this need, the leaders in the ecumenical movement at the Oxford Conference on Life and Work in 1937 recommended the establishment of Christian vocational fellowships which would bring together Christians in various vocations to consider their Christian duty in the specific situations faced in their work. This recommendation has issued in the development of such vocational groups in almost all the Protestant churches of Europe. The churches of the United States are only beginning to use this method of uniting the insights and values of Christian faith to the ethical complexities of many modern work situations.

As a means of assisting the Christian in his calling, Christian vocational fellowships have many advantages. First, the very existence of such a group witnesses to the fact that the Christian faith is meant to embrace the world. Secondly, because of individual participation in the solving process, problems can be approached from the uniquely personal perspective which problems have for each of us. Thirdly, the individual within the fellowship may not only make his specifically personal contribution but is able to benefit from the special talents of others who may possess unique experiences and insights. Fourthly, technical assistance and religious guidance to help clarify specific problems may be more easily secured by a group. Fifthly, where large areas of agreement are possible, greater confidence usually attends the conscience of the Christian. (The majority can, however, be wrong.) Sixthly, in situations of rapid change where new patterns emerge and elude the old standards of evaluation, the fellowship can be called to the new frontier to use its combined experience, judgment, and sensitized conscience to formulate an ethical opinion. The Christian vocational fellowship is a twentieth century social creation to meet twentieth century needs for the Christian in his vocation.

The development of Christian vocational fellowships for rural America is a pressing need if Protestantism wishes to preserve its creative social influence. Without assistance at many crucial points, the education, experience, and insight of the individual Christian prove to be insufficient to bring clarity and confidence to ethical decision.

But should Christian vocational fellowships be denominationally oriented, or should they be the creation to Protestant Christians working together in a Council of Churches? This question cannot be satisfactorily answered in principle apart from the peculiar situations of local areas. But it would appear that there would be more gained from ecumenically oriented groups than from denominational groups in the usual situation. In any event, the foregoing line of thought leads to the conclusion that Lutherans need to assume leadership in developing Christian vocational fellowships if they wish to free the individual Christian from confusion in the face of complexity so that the resources stemming from his faith might be released to form new social good from out of the midst of change.

III. Rural Fundamentalism and the Gospel

One of the most difficult obstacles confronting the attempt to relate Protestant beliefs and values to the emerging rural America is the deceptive attractiveness for Protestants of an outlook which has often been labeled as rural fundamentalism. This social fundamentalism upholds the superiority of the old rural life over city life, maintaining that it is a more natural way of life for man and produces people with better health and character. It is not only that the country air is better but old rural work arrangements and institutions are believed to be more satisfying and productive of better people.

The old rural community was organic in the sense that everyone was interrelated in deep ways. Personal tragedy or personal joy was shared by the community and a person was known as a whole being not separately as worker, club member, voter, father, or customer. In the old community, tradition spelled out what was right and wrong, proper or improper, and the community put its sanction on a folk ethic and folkways. The old rural community appreciated friendliness and was drawn closely enough together in personal contacts to bring a somewhat spontaneous community response to a wedding, a birth, a house raising, a death, property loss, etc. What we usually mean when we talk about the "good old days" is the good feeling that attended this way of life.

The relationship between Protestantism and this way of life has been more than incidental. Rural America has been settled in large part by white Protestants and the rural folk culture has been interpenetrated on every level by Protestant piety. The home, the church, and work were so interactive that it was hard to tell where the one began and the other ended. And in this social situation the intuitive response of the ethically educated individual conscience was more than not adequate. A form of Protestant ethic prevailed and was creative of good. It is not surprising that rural fundamentalism carries a nostalgic appeal for Protestants.

But this nostalgia can be dangerous for Protestantism as it faces a new rural situation and rural fundamentalism should be criticized, for the old rural life had many weaknesses as well as many strengths. Theologically, it is open to attack from a number of fronts. First, from the standpoint of the Lutheran concept of salvation by grace through faith, rural fundamentalism is theologically heretical because it tends to identify salvation with a particular social arrangement. The rural fundamentalist thinks that it is the organic society and the existence of wholesome personal relationships that make a man whole. The Lutheran must say to the Christless man of an organic society that he is not whole unless he is organically linked with the living Christ in the community of faith which is the church.

Secondly, judged by the Word of God the rural Protestant folk culture mistakenly legalized many of its customs and values as the absolute will of God. Rural-culture religion often identified what the community sanctioned with the ethical requirements of Christianity in the same way as contemporary culture religion (religion-in-general) identifies the requirements of the Sermon on the Mount with the dictates of the American way of life.

In addition to these theological criticisms, rural fundamentalism can be attacked by comparison of the benefits of the old way with the new. The result is by no means a one-sided ledger. The most obvious good which has come from the inclusion of agriculture into the industrialized economy is the tremendous increase in agricultural productivity which has made possible a more adequate diet for all. This has been accomplished by fewer and fewer people working fewer and fewer hours. New opportunities for enjoyment and self-development have been made possible by the increase in leisure. The new society into which the farmer has been introduced has provided more education for farm youth and has made possible, thereby, much upward mobility for those who have been forced to leave the rural area as a result of the increased technical efficiency of agriculture. The farmer and the townsman who depend upon agriculture have also shared in the advances in creature comforts made possible by industrialism. And modern medicine which is but another fruit of the whole technical revolution of which modern agriculture is a part has lengthened the lifespan of all. These are blessings which we ought not begrudge anyone.

The element of truth which exists in the position of the rural fundamentalist has to do with the preservation of an organic and personal approach to life without which some of the most important human potentialities cannot be realized. This is a cardinal truth and must stand before the eyes of those who daily are making the decisions which alter ways of living. From the Christian point of view an organic community and personal relationships are components of its picture of the ideal life under God in his kingdom of righteousness.

Where the fundamentalist errs (and this in a very fundamental way) is in believing that we can go back to life as it was. His romanticizing of the past and his sentimentalizing of old ways places him out of position to exert any appreciable influence on the developing rural society. Those who will play the most significant role in forming the social structure of the coming rural America are those whose fundamental orientation is to the future rather than the past. Protestantism must not romanticize its old rural role but must be oriented to the future and must seek to realize the values of the old way in whatever way and measure it is possible to realize them in the new situation. This point of view is justified, I think, by our Lutheran understanding of the doctrine of providence. The doctrine of providence, as Luther understood it, was not to lead us to bemoan our present situation but to accept it, not as the final summation of God's work (a view which would unjustifiably justify the *status quo*) but as that stage of it where he wishes us to work with him to realize more fully the potentialities of individuals and communities.

IV. Modern Farming and Christian Values

Modern American agriculture is not backward. The scientific accomplishments of the twentieth century are reflected there as are also the engineering developments involved in mechanization and mass production. The modern trend toward government participation in the economy as stimulator and regulator is perhaps most clearly seen in government farm programs and the manufacturing development toward larger and fewer units is traceable in rural America. Even the corporation form of business enterprise has made its appearance in farming. Rural work has become more like industrial work and rural life has many similarities to urban life. Country cousins may not have been first in every phase of modern endeavor but they have not been far behind and in their application of modern methods they have been eminently successful.

These developments of modern agriculture not only threaten old rural values which were associated with the old ways but they present new difficulties as well as new opportunities for the growth of values which are integrally related to Christian faith. An attempt will be made here only to mention some of these difficulties and opportunities.

Abundance and Christian Values

The most obvious place at which to begin is with the existence of abundance. As is indicated from the quotation from Luther which heads this essay, Paradise as a religious concept is not reserved for explaining the fulness of heaven or the bountiful character of a specific garden in the dim past. Paradise is the condition of abundance which belongs to all the earth as a blessing of God but can be lost through the evil machination of

1953\

men. As a concept it is intimately tied to the necessity of obedience to the righteous will of God, for the blessed Paradise can be turned into a cursed existence when man is forgetful of God.

Contrary to the mistaken but widely held view that Adam had to work only after his disobedience, the biblical view of Paradise included the labor of Adam who was to till the garden. He was commanded to be fruitful, which involved subduing the earth and gaining dominion over every living thing. Paradise was not a heavenly handout but the blessing of God upon the work of Adam as he subdued the earth and gained dominion over its living things. But Adam not only had to work, he was required to repose his trust in God and to obey his will. When Adam disobeyed, the blessing was removed and the difficulties developed.

The recognition of the hand of God in the fruitfulness of work is tied to a number of religious requirements. One of these obligations is thanksgiving. The Israelites were warned, "Beware lest you say in your heart, 'My power and the might of my hand have gotten me this wealth.' You shall remember the Lord your God, for it is he who gives you power to get wealth. . ." Deut. 8:17, 18. Without the hand of God nothing can succeed and it is a religious requirement to offer him thanks and obey his will.

One of the difficulties in modern farming is in the recognition of the real basis for thanksgiving. Scientific farming has been accompanied for many people by a religion of scientism which is a modern way of saying that the might of my brain and the power of my hand has gotten these things for me. The rapid increase in the power of man to subdue the earth and have dominion over its living things has brought some to the Promethean affirmation that man is king of the universe. This is a far different thing from subduing the earth and exercising dominion over its creatures under the sovereign power of a righteous God.

It is the responsibility of the Christian church to remind the modern farmer that modern science and production methods cannot guarantee abundance. The human idolatry in scientism

Lincoln Christian College

corrupts man and society and issues in expulsion from Paradise. The power of man to create good has brought with it the equivalent power to destroy.

Lutheran faith does not believe that an economy of scarcity is more religious. Abundance it conceives as a blessing of God upon the faithful and loving labor of man. The scientific and engineering goal of gaining power over the earth and its living things it approves as a command of God. But scientism which exploits the pride of man, it sees as the construct of evil.

Another of the threats to the values integrally related to Christian faith particularly present in the economy of abundance is the life of materialism. High productivity, not only on the farm but in the factory, has required high consumption. Advertising, which is not a new invention, has, however, become a pervasive feature of American life since the advent of mass production and keeps an unrelenting pressure upon us to get more things. Our abundance has not yet, at least, let us look at the possession of things with the detachment of the "old rich." Far from alleviating our anxieties about what we shall eat and what we shall wear, our abundance has been dominated by the philosophy that meaning and status are intimately related to the things which we possess.

There are many distortions of Christian value in the present materialism. First, it tends to confuse the role of man. The extreme emphasis upon the importance of consumption diminishes the importance of man's role as the producer of good. Secondly, it tends to substitute the possession of things for the values of self-development. At times it even equates the two. Thirdly, it deceives us by inciting a false security in us like the rich man of Scripture who told himself to take his ease because he had many goods stored up. Basically, materialism is a distortion of life because it is a faithless response to abundance and thereby fails to put material values in their proper perspective.

In order to keep man free from the corruption of materialism, the Christian Church must make clear in manifold ways the steward philosophy of life. Stewardship is materialistic only in the sense that it appreciates the benefits of things and the good that things can do. But stewardship challenges the supposition of a materialistic philosophy that the meaning of life consists of the possession of things. Stewardship acknowledges that all we have is of God and that the material blessings of life are to be used as the undergirding for personal and community development. Christian stewardship conscientiously pursued is a faithful response to abundance which keeps the use of abundance subject to the aims of God in working with men and communities.

Farm Work and Christian Values

Some observers of the modern farm have detected tendencies toward dehumanization, depersonalization and devaluation in the application of the life sciences, mass production methods, and modern commercial procedures to agriculture. They say that there is a loss of human sympathy with the sensate world in the way "Animals (are) lined up like machines, bred like mechanisms, and pushed to ever higher and higher levels of production."[4] They note that as man invests less of himself and more of a machine in his work that he has less personal appreciation for the products of his labor. And they point out that government agencies and bank managers have more to say about what crops will be grown and what methods will be used than the man who does the farming. Yearly the number of important decisions the individual farmer can make by himself diminishes. The old individualism of the farmer has given way, they say, to the team approach. The modern farmer is developing the same sort of values as the corporation man.

These conclusions appear to this observer to be overdrawn. That there are tendencies in this direction will not, however, be denied, but agriculture has been spared the worst effects of these tendencies because of its nature. The factory system has been much more subject to these ills than farming. There is much more dehumanization, depersonalization and devaluation on a noisy assembly line than on a combine, or in a modern milking barn. And the dealings of the individual farmer with the banker or the farm agent allow much more participation in the work decisions than the worker on the assembly line has.

Much of the continuing interest of the farmer in his work derives from its variety and constant challenge to resourcefulness as well as from his need to keep abreast of the advances being made in the many scientific fields related to his work. And where the family farm still prevails, farming continues to be a way of life rather than an eight hour job. A large number of midwestern farmers are related to a village or small town community in which they are known personally. Pride in farm projects is revealed in the stock shows and county fairs. There are many evidences that farming remains as a satisfying way of life not untouched but largely uncorrupted by the work changes introduced by modern farm methods. The major affront to the soul in most midwest farming comes not so much from farm methods as from the demoralizing effects of subsistence living either for the farmer on a marginal farm, or for exploited farm help.

The value of the reverence for life, however, is the value which seems to be threatened most by new farm methods and outlooks. This value is integrally related to Christian faith and was uniquely and forcefully set forth by Luther in his understanding of the relation of God to nature. One of the fruits of a well-developed Lutheran piety should be deep appreciation for the sacredness of all life. This Lutheran expression of reverence for life is not romanticism or nature mysticism but is derivative from Luther's concept of the omnipresence of God. While Luther held to the idea of the personality of God, he divested the characterization of God from anthropomorphism. God was not localized in a heaven making occasional sorties into the world of space and time but was everywhere present, not in a distended fashion, but fully, personally present everywhere, in, with, around, and under all things.

This was not pantheism because God was transcendent over the world of space and time as well. God, Luther held, was consubstantially related to all things. The thing itself was not divine but was intimately related to the divine. Creatures, including man, did not participate in divinity but were sacredly related to the God who lived in them.

All creatures are the masks of God and God can be seen in them and through them by the person who sees them through the eyes of biblical faith. According to Luther, God has chosen to be known personally only through his Word, but the person who knows him through his Word can also see him and honor him in his creation. In this sense nature is alive with God for Lutheran piety. But this understanding of the sanctity of nature does not confuse the relationship of creature to Creator by investing creatures with divinity, nor does it confuse the lordship of man over nature by making things or dumb creatures the possessors of divine substance. For the Lutheran the sanctity that inheres in nature is not profaned when man is able to increase the usefulness of things and animals by a more perceptive understanding of nature. The sanctity of nature is lost for the Lutheran when he fails to see the hand and presence of God in the marvel of the new productivity.

The understanding of the sanctity of life does not leave the creation without rights or man without a sense of what is proper in dealing with creation. Beauty has its place as well as usefulness and is to be cultivated because God who leads in creative activity makes the world not only useful but filled with beauty—and gentleness is a Christian virtue that is to be cultivated as an attitude of life toward all things. Specific injunctions against cruelty to animals is part of the biblical law. The lordship of man in creation is inextricably linked in Christian understanding with ethical constraints which guard against exploitation.

The values which inhere in Christian faith have always been threatened. Modern life introduces new conditions for life, however, which accentuate many old threats and add some new ones. Since the Christian does not live in a religiously or ethically neutral world, he must be on guard to detect and give battle to that which would destroy his faith and the quality of life which it produces.

V. Guidelines from Lutheran Teaching for the Christian in His Work and Community Role

In conclusion it appears to be more appropriate to set forth guidelines than to summarize the various approaches made thus far. Through this means, it is hoped, it will be possible to pull together some of the scattered theological themes registered in the course of these remarks. It is also hoped that the statement of guidelines will make it possible to apply insights and values deriving from Lutheran faith to many areas not even touched by the explorations made herein.

The Life of the Christian Must Be Priestly

The evangelical Christian understands that he is saved by God's grace which is appropriated by faith. Since salvation is a gift, his life must be a grateful response to this gift which involves the dedication of life to the service of God and man. Through faith he knows that what he does in faith and out of love is accepted by God as a spiritual service rendered to him. The whole life, then, of the Christian, including his family, work, and civic duties are to be offered as a spiritual service to God. This is the priestly function of the Christian.

The Life of the Christian Must Be Prophetic

The Christian is not only called to offer his work to God but to resist everything which is contrary to the will of God. Through God's law and in the understanding of life which is given in the experience of love, man is given a plumb line by which to judge the straightness of the structures of life. It is man's duty as a servant of God to test the straightness of the social structures in which he lives and to work for the removal of error by every means appropriate to the law of God and the situation in need of correction.

The Life of the Christian Must Be Public

God is not only the Creator of persons but also of peoples and nations. Extreme individualism which fails to recognize the public responsibilities of each person is a distortion of the biblical view of man. The Christian must not only thank God for the community in which he finds his earthly fellowship but must work with God to build and preserve community against the forces which would destroy it. This does not mean that outworn communities are to be kept alive when their usefulness is no longer apparent. It does mean that the Christian must help to create new and better community when communities are changing.

The Life of the Christian Must Be Personal

The crown of God's creation is the person. While God is personally interrelated with the whole creation, only man is capable of communion with God. From one point of view all of creation is to serve the development of the person who is its crown. This special dignity is a gift of God to man. That which demeans, debases, or debilitates the person is to be resisted. That which edifies, ennobles, enlightens, or inspires the person must be promoted.

The Life of the Christian Must Be Psychologically Therapeutic

This is another way of saying that the Christian is to recover that wholeness of life which is destroyed when we center life too much about ourselves. Christian wisdom holds that when we die to self, we arise to new and fuller life. By involvement in tasks which involve denial of self in order to serve others, it is possible to recover some psychological wholeness. Only when life is a mission is there a sufficient integrative center to provide dynamic and form for the development of all of the potentialities of man. This Christian wisdom must be proclaimed by the Church as belonging to the heart of the Gospel and all personal and social conditions which militate against the conception of life as a mission must be countered.

The Life of the Christian Must Be Productive

Does the necessity to conceive of life as a mission mean that the Christian man must pursue his work with a passionate religious zeal? The answer to this is both a "yes" and a "no." Affirmatively viewed it means that the Christian must appreciate the social importance of his work, uphold its dignity and value, and fulfill his responsibilities to it with honesty and integrity. Negatively considered, it does mean that the old vocational virtues of unrelenting diligence and consistent thrift no longer apply to the economy of abundance in the same way that they were relevant to an economy of scarcity. The age of abundance requires some social control of work to prevent wasted production and also as a means to secure dignified employment for all. The mission of the individual is related to the mission of his society.

FOOTNOTES

[1]Kepler, Thomas, ed., *The Table Talk of Martin Luther,* The World Publishing Company, 1952, p. 79.

[2]Pelikan, Jaroslav, ed., *Luther's Works,* Vol. 1. Concordia Publishing House, St. Louis, 1958, p. 212.

[3]Brunner, Emil, *The Divine Imperative,* Trans. Olive Wyon, The Westminster Press, Philadelphia, 1947, p. 189.

[4]Pollard, William G., "The Relation of the Christian College to the Scientific World," p. 5. An address delivered to the First Quadrennial Convocation of Christian Colleges in 1954.

9.

COMMUNITY
DEVELOPMENT

Mid-America is in the midst of an intense interest in community development. Awakening to the sociological effects of the rapid advances in technology, individuals, institutions, and governments have expressed deep concern for the effects of change upon the community. In mid-America these changes threaten the existence of institutions in communities primarily dependent upon an agricultural economy. Technological changes in agriculture have made possible a sharp reduction in the number of individuals needed for production of food and fiber. Institutions which minister to persons rather than industries are particularly affected by the changes now occurring. The churches in rural areas are keenly aware of the impact of population shifts brought about by technological advances.

Individuals, institutions, and governments are inquiring into the possibilities and potentialities of community development. The extent to which these possibilities may be realized will be determined by the degree to which communities are willing to make significant adjustments in their community life.

Two major philosophies of community development prevail. There are those who equate community development with community action toward the achievement of specific objectives. Others see community development as a process through which the citizens are educated as they participate in analyzing situations, preparing alternatives, deciding upon a course of action and finally in participating in the action phase of the program. This view ultimately includes action, but gives greater emphasis to the educational process through involvement in the community development activity.

When community development is viewed as an action program to accomplish a specific task then the means of accomplishment are selected on that basis. However, if community development is viewed as an educational process then the means to be used are selected with a two-fold purpose. The means selected are to educate the participants and to achieve the objectives desired.

Carl C. Taylor has condensed and refined Edward Lindeman's nine stages in the community development process into the following four stages:

1. ... A systematic discussion of common-felt needs by members of the community.

2. ... A systematic plan to carry out the first self-help undertaking that has been selected by the community.

3. ... Almost complete mobilization and harnessing of the physical, economic, and social potentialities of local community groups.

4. ... Creation of aspiration and the determination to undertake additional community improvement projects.

Education of the participants is an important part of each of the four above stages. Efficiency in the learning process can be increased with competent leadership—both volunteer and professional, and the education and leadership development of the citizens participating will contribute significantly to the effectiveness of the democratic process in the community.

If the community development process is to operate effectively and efficiently three conditions must exist:

First, any action must be community centered. The prime purpose of the community development process is to educate the participating citizens and to achieve worthwhile objectives bene-

ficial to the entire community. Interest will be higher and the
efforts will be greater if the problems to be solved derive from
genuine felt needs of the immediate community.

Secondly, the community must be means oriented. Emphasis
is given to the means rather than the ends because of the importance of the educational aspects of the community development process in relation to our democratic principles and the
development of leadership for our democracy.

Last, community action must have a functional structure. If
successful social action is to occur then an appropriate organizational structure must be established. However, the structure
must never become the end but must always remain a part of
the means in the process.

Leadership in the community development process is of extreme importance. This is true whether the leaders are volunteers or professionals. Ordway Tead has defined leadership as
"the activity of helping people work together toward a chosen
goal."

Five primary characteristics of an effective leader in community development are: acceptance, a desire to lead, the personality to do the job, a knowledge of the community and its
problems, and skills in working with people.

Acceptance of the leader by the group requires that the leader
is identified as a person of integrity, is respected, is able to establish and maintain rapport with all members of the group, and is
capable of articulating not only his concerns and philosophy,
but also the concerns and beliefs of the group with whom he
serves.

A desire to lead is an important characteristic of a leader.
However, in community development this desire to lead must
be genuinely in the interests of the group. In selecting a leader,
or leaders in community development, those making the selection need to be confident that the desire to lead is directed toward the best interests of the community.

Together with a desire to lead, a leader in community development must have the personality to do the job. Desirable per-

sonality traits are loyalty to those whom he serves, stature, poise, the ability to communicate, and the ability to articulate clearly the needs, the alternatives, and the goals to be achieved.

Knowledge of the community, its residents, the problems to be solved, and the techniques for community development is another high priority characteristic required of the leaders in community development.

The leader in community development must have the skills necessary for working with people. Such skills include the ability to plan a meeting, preside at meetings using proper parliamentary procedures, planning and conducting discussions and working with groups and committees.

Qualified leaders and representative groups who undertake community development activities need to understand how social action takes place in a community.

Before social action occurs in a community some individual, individuals, or groups who understand the social system of the community and who are aware of prior social situations will initiate limited action relating to needs of the community. Continuance of this limited action will depend largely upon legitimation of the idea or proposal by the people of the community. When legitimation of the social action contemplated is secured the proposal is diffused to a larger segment of the community. This action awakens the community to the need for action dealing with this problem. When sufficient awareness of the need exists then a decision to act is made. Following this decision, goals are determined, means are selected for achieving the goals and a plan of attack on the problem is established. The leaders and the key groups are now ready to mobilize and organize their resources and carry out the program designed to achieve the stated goal or objectives. Throughout the entire social action process each step is evaluated and refined as necessary for the successful social action. When one action is completed the leaders and the community serve the need for a similar attack on other community needs. Once community development is initiated in a community and a substantial proportion of the citizens become involved and educated in the process, community development becomes a continuum.

Community development has received encouragement from governmental units. The Federal Government, through its encouragement of Rural Areas Development, has stimulated many communities to action in solving their own community problems.

Rural Areas Development, a government approach, is a form for community development in which the community consists of the whole county and will very likely encompass a number of communities. Viewing the county as a single community has reduced some of the intense competition among individual small municipalities and has enabled them to cooperate in community development on a broader scale and has facilitated cooperative efforts in development of the large community, the county. This larger area approach has enabled some communities to specialize in the services they render to the larger community. In mid-America, community development as carried on under Rural Areas Development assists communities to adjust to changes more effectively, and actually develop successfully within the greater community.

The modus operandi or structure for Rural Areas Development is similar to that used in community development activities. Basically, this structure consists of a committee representative of all phases of the society in the community. This committee known as the steering committee, takes a critical look at the county analyzing its needs, lifting up its problem areas, studying alternatives for solving the problems, and drafting a proposal for goals to be achieved.

Extensive use is made of subcommittees gathering data and proposing possibilities and goals in specific areas of concern. These committees report to the steering committee and work together in approving the final plan for county—community development. In the Rural Areas Development approach this is known as the O.E.D.P.—the Overall Economic Development Program.

One of the keys to a successful Rural Areas Development plan is the involvement of a large number of persons representing a true cross section of the community. Their involvement becomes an educational experience and also becomes a commitment to improve their community.

Rural Areas Development is an educational process resulting in the adjustment of the resources, human and material, to bring about community development. The educational and organizational responsibilities of Rural Areas Development are the responsibility of the Cooperative Extension Service within the United States Department of Agriculture. The leadership in the counties consists of capable volunteers who have a deep interest in community development, who are accepted and respected, who have the capacity to motivate others to assist them in guiding this form of community development.

Reference was made earlier to the keen interest of the church in community development. The churches in mid-America have evidenced deep concern about the rapidly changing communities and the allocation of the church resources that should be made to minister most effectively to these changing communities. The churches have a responsibility for assisting with the community development process, both as a witnessing church in the community and as a social institution providing dedicated Christian persons to participate in the community development process.

The concern of the church for the fullest development of the individual as a Christian witnessing in his community necessitates a comparable concern for the healthy development of the community in which the individual lives and the church ministers. Concern for the development of a wholesome healthy community—economically, educationally, socially, politically and religiously is a responsibility of the church if those to whom it ministers are to have opportunity to fulfill their role in life.

This concern of the church can be evidenced in several ways in community development. The most effective leadership a church can give is to provide competent dedicated men and women to give leadership in community development. The role of the church in community development need not be a direct one with the pastor stating the position of the church on each issue discussed, but rather, the role of the church might be more significant through the lay leadership referred to earlier.

The church in mid-America needs to be alert to its opportunities to make significant contributions in community development. This is an educational process that will equip churchmen to fulfill more completely the responsibilities as concerned citizens in a democratic society. The church has an obligation and an opportunity to equip those to whom it ministers to carry out these responsibilities.

Community development is not new in the United States or the world, but it has become a matter of intense concern in mid-America at this point in history. The success of positive community development in educating the participants and achieving the objectives will have a marked impact on the continuance of our democratic society.

II.
The
Church
Speaks

10.

MINISTERING TO PEOPLE
IN TOWN AND COUNTRY

The vital question facing the church in mid-America today is how can the church most effectively witness to and serve people in the rapidly changing town and country communities?

Some communities are growing rapidly. Others are declining with equal speed, and some are precariously managing to maintain a relatively stable population. The make-up of the people in communities of all sizes is changing. More of their population are in the older age brackets due to increased longevity. Fewer young people have the opportunity to enter farming. In many small communities businesses which once flourished have seen economic and technological changes draw both farm and nonfarm customers to larger centers of trade.

Since most communities and congregations were located and developed before the turn of the century it follows that both the communities and their churches are being greatly affected by this change in mobility. Most congregations, in what we now call the town and country area, were established during the days of what has been described as the "horse-drawn technology." In the time once needed to travel five miles a person today can easily travel fifty by means of the automobile and modern highways.

New machines and new products have been accepted and encouraged by people living on farms and in rural communities. When automobiles and trucks were developed people wanted them and bought them. Hard surfaced highways have come to be as desired in rural areas as in the city. The mechanization of farm production was brought about and machines replaced men and horses. The accumulative affects of these and other influences have changed the characteristics of trade and service centers. When new technological developments are accepted, it is necessary to accept and deal with the resulting changes.

A single community, or even a single county, is no longer adequate as a basic economic and social unit. As I have said, most small communities were established in the days of horse-drawn transportation and counties were laid out during the same period. It was then thought that a county should be of such size that any resident could travel to the county seat, transact his business and return to his home in the same day.

Iowa counties, for example, are generally about 576 square miles, and include about 16 townships. The developing pattern of rural life now dictates that a functional rural area in mid-America be about ten times that of the typical county. Such an "area" has a "central city" with a population ranging from 25,000 to 100,000, and also has "satellite towns." The area includes about 5,000 square miles, about 8 or 9 counties and a population of about 250,000. Such economic and social areas are becoming recognized. In dealing with the ministry of the church in this emerging town and country society it is necessary to understand these larger emerging areas.[1] The growth of these areas has been brought about by many interrelated forces. The changes in transportation, mechanization and scientific developments are major factors. When opportunities decreased in farming, businesses and industries developing in the central city and satellite towns supplied employment and helped maintain an acceptable level of living. Higher income opportunities caused people to commute from country areas to jobs in distant communities.

If the church is to fulfill its mission of ministering to the emerging town and country society it must know the larger community as it is and as what it is becoming. A purely senti-

mental view of rural life is inadequate. To overcome the gap
which exists between the community and congregation structures of times past and the community and congregation structures of today the church needs to recognize the realities of
change and seek to understand the factors at work and be willing to make the necessary adjustments. Where a merger of congregations is advisable, congregations should have the courage
to bring about such a merger. Where the withdrawal of a congregation will strengthen the witness of the church, orderly
withdrawal should be sought. Where a new congregation is
needed in a growing or unserved area, it should be established.

The Role of the Pastor

The pastor's role centers in and emanates from the office of
the ministry. The pastor is the spiritual shepherd for the people of the parish. The fostering and nurturing of Christian faith
among people is his calling. Incorporated in this task is a concern for the whole man. The whole man is a person with relationships to his family, his church, his community and his occupation. The pastor must understand the layman's needs if he
is to help him meet his responsibility in these relationships.

Young people need pastors who are effective spiritual coun-
selors and guides. The Christian education of children and youth
through parish education, confirmation and youth organizations
calls for understanding and devotion. In the foundation of
Christian faith youth have "a good work" begun in them. They
need help in their development as Christian persons. They need
help as they think about the occupations and professions which
they may enter. This is especially important in a changing situation where young people are not likely to follow in the occupational footsteps of their parents.

The pastor must keep aware of occupational opportunities in
order to conduct a helpful conversation with the youth of his
parish. This can be done through literature of educational and
occupational agencies and through various study conferences.

The pastor has an opportunity to help youth recognize the contribution they can make through particular occupations or professions. When a pastor is closely associated with young people and they share with him their various educational and occupatonal experiences it gives breadth of interest to his ministry. This is true when young people remain in the community as well as when they disperse through the country and the world. Schools and youth organizations can also help young people discover career opportunities. Through discussions with the local school's guidance counselor and youth organization leaders, the pastor can learn more about occupations and about young people and their aspirations.

Self-study of a congregation is another area in which the pastor can help people to understand changes and needs which affect their congregation. How well do members know and live the Christian faith? What are the age levels of the members in comparison with the age levels of the community? How effective is Christian education in the parish? How well are the spiritual and physical needs of people being met? How well is the physical plant being used?   What is the congregation's influence in the community? Is the congregation helping to bring Christian charity and the Gospel to all people? These are some of the questions the congregation must ask itself if it is to be helpful to the community.

Community changes and the relationship of the community to larger economic and social areas should also command the attention of the pastor. The extent of involvement in community self-study and development may best be determined by the pastor himself. In most cases showing a genuine interest in the efforts of laymen is sufficient. However, in some instances a pastor may do well to become more directly involved. In all cases his efforts should be directed toward helping laymen to develop a sense of responsibility and leadership.

In the emerging society the pastor has the opportunity and responsibility to exemplify the concern of the church for the well-being of people and the community. When he limits his concern and interest to immediate members of his congregation, he restricts the influence of the church. In his concern for the well-being of people in the community, the pastor needs to be aware that a relationship exists between himself and individuals. He also has a relationship with the community as a whole. Recognition of the significance of these relationships is important for the pastor. By thoughtful interest, understanding, and encouragement, the pastor can contribute to the wholesome development of both the individual and the community.

The Role of the Layman

If a congregation is to minister to a changing community, then the layman has an essential role. The role of the layman has roots in two facts: He is a member of the Christian church and he is a member of the community. In the layman the church and community meet. To be responsible in his dual role he must contribute through both thought and action.

The layman needs to demonstrate what it means to be a Christian in a congregation. He needs to know the law and gospel of Christian faith as relevant forces in his life and in the lives of others. He has a responsibility to help the congregation to which he belongs be a useful force in ministering to the spiritual and physical needs of people. When changing community patterns develop he should help his congregation to adjust in order to minister more effectively to people in the emerging situation. This may involve a merger with another congregation, moving a church building into an appropriate community or it may even mean withdrawing a congregation from the community altogether. In some situations the realignment of congregations is as important to laymen of today as starting congregations was to laymen of 75 or 100 years ago.

The layman must also demonstrate what it means to be a Christian in a community. He must recognize the need to bear witness in public life. In cultural, economic, educational, political and social affairs he can study the issues and develop his thinking. When reasonably confident that he can make a constructive contribution, he can communicate his ideas in public meetings and in personal conversations. Demonstrating a Christian concern includes a willingness to work and give leadership when and where it is needed. Responses to a questionnaire from over 300 council members of Lutheran congregations in mid-America indicated that 95 per cent thought responsible involvement in public affairs was an important function of a Christian. Every layman concerned about his community, state and nation will regard it a duty and privilege to study the political issues and vote according to his conclusions. When called on to run for public office he should enter the political process with a sense of obligation and opportunity for service.

The Role of the Congregation

The first task of the congregation is to provide the people of the parish and community with a meaningful service of worship. In the service of worship, God's grace and counsel are communicated through Word and Sacrament. A congregation should be concerned that its worship service is meaningful and available to all people.

The congregation is responsible for parish education for children, youth and adults. This includes the preparation of teachers for the church school. Study meetings and parish education conferences sponsored by the church body are means by which the congregation can strengthen its parish education.

An alert congregation ought to be concerned with the immediate community and the larger area in which it is located. Through worship and parish education the congregation can minister to people and bear witness to the Christian faith in the community. The congregation will consciously acquaint itself with the changes in the society in which it ministers and seek to share its constructive influence.

In view of population shifts and changes within the communities of a larger area, the congregation needs to deal with overchurching when and where it develops. Where consolidation or mergers can result in a more adequate use of resources, congregations should advance the mission of the church by taking the necessary action.

Realignments need to be based on a careful study of the situation. Members of congregations and parishes should help to gather the information and should have sufficient time to discuss the issues and make decisions as to the best use of the church's resources in the light of the mission of the church in the community. Consolidation of congregations and parishes can be beneficial and successful when the decision to consolidate grows out of understanding. The process of decision making by the people is as important as the consolidation itself. When consolidation takes place it is well to make provision for those things which have heartfelt meaning to people, such as a church building that is no longer needed.

The Role of the Church Body

The presidents of jurisdictional units, such as districts and synods, are the leaders of the church bodies who are closest to the congregations and parishes. These leaders have a concern for the people, congregations and parishes. Just as a pastor needs helpful insights from farmers and businessmen in his community, jurisdictional leaders need to be informed about the changes, needs and problems in the emerging town and country society. Both laymen and pastors can share information with their leaders concerning farm and rural community changes and problems.

Leaders of a church body can help to create the proper climate for the study of congregations and parishes. This can be accomplished by discussing the mission of the church in the community with laymen and pastors. By concern, interest and discussion, jurisdictional leaders can help in the process of study and in the making of important decisions.

Parish effectiveness is related to many factors. Some of these are size of congregation, size of church school, location of a church building, salary of the pastor, the pastor's parish travel provision, etc. What is the future of a congregation if its baptized membership remains less than 300; if its church school enrollment remains less than 100; if the pastor's salary is less than $4,800; or if there is an inadequate provision for parish travel? The jurisdictional leader should discuss these factors with congregations or arrange to have the congregation study them under competent guidance. A study group of local members can also suggest new approaches for their ministry.

A study group may suggest that several congregations develop joint programs which will complement their ministry and make wiser use of their resources. Some study groups have suggested a joint parish education program, a coordinated youth program and an area counseling service for congregations of a community. Together the congregations can provide the administration, facilities and staff. Leaders of church bodies can assist congregations to develop broader approaches to meet needs and opportunities in a changing scene.

FOOTNOTE

[1]For a fuller discussion of the "area" and "central city" concepts the reader may wish to study "Delineating the Area," by Dr. Karl A. Fox, a paper presented at the Conference on Area Development, January 8-10, 1962, at Athens, Georgia. Also, "The Study of Interactions Between Agriculture and the Nonfarm Economy: Local, Regional, and National," by Dr. Karl A. Fox, Journal of Farm Economics, Vol. XLIV, No. 1, February, 1962.

11.

DEVELOPING ESSENTIAL
LEADERSHIP

On a night airplane flight over mid-America one can look down on a constellation of lighted places, and each concentration of light is a Farmville, mid-America. Few people know it well, if at all, because Farmville is located in every county and in almost every township, of the region. The pilot may tell his passengers about Des Moines or Omaha, nearly everyone knows these cities, but there are many Farmvilles.

The emerging town and country society is made up of thousands of such towns, each with its own past and future. Their populations may range from a few hundred to several thousand.

From the vantage point of an airliner these many small towns may seem quite isolated, and indeed once they were. Yet in our lifetime we have seen them become firmly linked to the rest of the nation, and as much in contact with American life as any large city. As the cliché has it, small towns are very much alike, yet today their similarity is of a different kind, and they may be identified far more easily by their common problems than by their mutual successes. And these common problems can perhaps be best summed up in one question: "What is going to happen to our town in the future?"

A keystone in the future life of every community is its leadership. An alert, informed and capable leadership is essential for planning and guiding each of the thousands of small towns. The development of leadership merits the attention of society, both church and state, in our time.

Why Leadership Development Is Important

At a time when communities, whatever their size, are being shaken by economic trends, population shifts and technological developments, community goals are necessary to provide direction. Worthwhile achievements do not just happen, they are planned for. Unified effort is needed to bring them about, and in order to secure a unified effort one must have leadership.

A large portion of the American population lives in the numerous small communities of the emerging town and country society. The extent to which the rural population exercises the rights and responsibilities of citizenship depends, to a large extent, upon its leadership.

Education and employment are just two areas of great national concern. To provide a high quality of education for rural youth is the duty of every community. To provide training in the expanding technical skills, and retraining for employees displaced by technological change, is another. Yet to accomplish goals such as these the community must have capable leadership to direct its work.

Other factors also indicate the need for leadership. Unsolved social and economic problems exist in both healthy and declining communities. With the development of industry and the increase in the numbers of rural nonfarm people, rural zoning may require the attention of the community. The growing acceptance of the concepts and functions of community development provide new opportunities for leadership. The tension being experienced between commercial farming and the processing industry points to a need for constructive leadership on both sides. The apportionment of political representation in rural and urban areas emphasizes the need for political information and guidance. With the new importance of communities between 5,000 and 25,000 as service centers, smaller communities need to develop their services to complement, rather than compete with, these larger cities.

Parish development by congregations calls for lay and pastoral leadership. While businesses and social institutions (for example, farm implement dealers and health clinics) have organized to serve an area rather than one small community, some congregations have not developed their programs to serve on a larger scale. Businesses and social agencies in many cases have realigned their programs to improve their service and make better use of their resources. Information is needed on the economic and social changes that will take place in the future, as well as knowledge of the changes which have already occurred. Parish self-study and planning present opportunities and responsibilities in many rural areas.

Soil scientists and foresters plan shelter belts of trees according to land use, and the study of the nature of soil and climatic conditions in specific areas to prevent erosion by wind and water. In a like manner, leaders of rural society, with the help of social scientists, need to plan the community's social agencies and institutions to conserve the strength of people and their resources.

Where Leadership Once Grew

Before the agricultural revolution and World War II uprooted rural society, leadership evolved within special social groups. Family and kinship circles were a prominent social element in many farm areas. They were focal points for personal identification. They met individual, family and group needs through mutual consideration, and certain members emerged as spokesmen and leaders. Today relatively few such circles exert the influence or develop the leaders they once did.

Formerly neighborhood ties were strong in open country and small towns. Neighborliness and neighborhoods developed during decades and generations of association and the meeting of common dangers and problems. In these neighborhoods some individuals came to be recognized as leaders and were looked to for their ability. But now modern transportation and communication methods have lessened dependence on neighborhood leaders.

Ethnic groups were common in many areas only a few decades ago. Those who were first to learn the English language and new ways gave leadership in relating their group to the new country. Other members led their groups in common cultural concerns. Ethnic groups no longer serve a major function in rural life. The Americanization of such groups, as well as economic and social mobility, have greatly reduced this type of influence, and this source for the development of leadership is disappearing.

How the Church Can Help

Congregations in town and country areas can share in the development of leadership. The concern of the church should be beyond itself. Self-preservation and institutional success, though admirable, ought never be considered all-important. The church must give itself to the world, and more particularly to the community. Greatness in service as portrayed in the parable of the Good Samaritan is the goal to which the church has been called. In seeking this goal the church can take hold of its responsibility by helping to develop leadership.

But how is the church to take part in the development of leadership? Through its message, the church influences the life and thought of people. Where this message of the church is received, concern for the well-being of others replaces complacency. Awareness to social needs and problems can be encouraged. Self-interest is reduced to its proper size and interest in the community increases. The Christian exerts a constructive unifying influence instead of being divisive. These characteristics—concern, awareness, community interest, constructive influence—are some of the necessary qualities for leadership which the church must encourage.

Congregations can help to develop leadership by learning to know more about what it is and how to employ it more responsibly. Social scientists have made thorough studies of leadership. The information they share can help congregations deepen their understanding of it. In a survey of 300 church council men in mid-American congregations, 96%, indicated that they thought the development of leadership important. But the responses also indicate that there is less certainty on how to do it.

Qualities necessary for becoming a leader exist in individuals in all communities. By learning to know more of the characteristics of leadership, congregations can make a greater contribution to its development. Sometimes leadership does not express itself. Congregations should consider recruiting both interest and experience.

Leadership training schools are offered both by educational institutions and by church agencies. A congregation should encourage and assist the potential leaders it may recruit to attend such schools. Community organizations, as well as the organizations of a congregation, provide ready opportunity for putting leadership training to use. As the individual leaders in a congregation gain experience and insight they need to be encouraged to assume leadership responsibilities in society.

The future of the town and country society greatly depends on the leaders it can develop, for without them progress will be very difficult.

12.

COMMUNICATING THE CHRISTIAN MESSAGE

A brief discussion of the communication of the Christian message in changing town and country communities runs risks, for it takes for granted what is communication. It largely assumes what is the Christian message. It deals too easily and quickly with a demanding process.

What Is Involved?

God is the sender of the Christian message into the stirring town and country society. He is not thwarted by changes on the human scene. Cultural, social and technological changes are, in fact, undergirded by the possibilities which he gives in creation. Change is a product of man at work in the setting of time What concerns the God is the spirit, purpose and values man holds in bringing about the adjustment to change.

God has given his message to man. That message was entrusted to the prophets and apostles who themselves lived in societies confronted by problems of food and fiber production, cultural influences and population shifts. What determines the character of life is not the struggle but the spirit; the purpose and values with which man enters the struggle. The message entrusted to the prophets and apostles is precisely the same message to be communicated in changing town and country communities. While the message is the same the applications are new, for man has never before moved into the expansive technological arena now being entered.

In the changing town and country society the Christian message has as many targets as there are people, and some identification of the classifications of the people in the region can be helpful.

There are farm people, some of whom are in commercial farming. Their farms vary in size, specialization and net income. They may own, lease or rent their land. They may be young farmers entering a highly capitalized business or those well along in years, farming land which was bought rather inexpensively decades ago. There are part-time farmers in the region. There are also some marginal farmers who produce relatively little and whose income is meager.

Rural nonfarm people, in their increasing numbers, comprise a considerable shifting population group. They are both white-collar workers and blue-collar workers. (Of four rural nonfarm families in an Illinois community, interviewed recently by a layman, two had never been visited by a layman or a pastor of any local congregation. Both of the families had lived in the community for over four years.)

Numerous people with inadequate incomes live in mid-America communities. They struggle for existence and for meaning in life. Many of them are aged. The average age of people in rural areas is rising. (Iowa, for example, has the highest per cent of aged people in the nation.) There are more people over the age of 50 who are not members of a congregation than in any other age bracket. Unemployment or underemployment affects persons of all ages. Fast moving economic trends have often taken away the opportunity to earn a decent living and there is a high incidence of people who need welfare support in rural communities. People may be deprived of a sense of worth due to inadequate income, poverty or dependence on others.

Some people of considerable means—businessmen, professional people and others—live in rural communities. They are economically independent and socially self-sufficient. They are secure. Perhaps they "couldn't care less" that there is a Christian message.

School dropouts and unemployed youth make up yet another group of people who are in need of receiving something of value. The delinquency rate of youth in rural areas is rising at a more rapid rate than in other parts of American society. The problems of rural youth in a changing environment have national implications.

Yet many people do not fit into any of the above groupings. They are in too many classifications to list separately. They make up the majority of the small community population, are long-term residents and have a wide diversity of occupations. Their existence may not be threatened but they are thinking about the implications of trends and future changes. They may or may not be members of a congregation.

Farmers, rural nonfarm people, those with inadequate incomes, the wealthy, rural youth and the long-term small town residents —these are the people in changing town and country communities whom God intends to be receivers of the Christian message.

The Church Is the Communicator

The church is the channel through which God intends to communicate his message to people in changing communities. The Christian message is sent to the church to receive and to share it. However for the church to receive the Christian message it must be listening for his Word.

A congregation exists to build and to serve people. People do not exist to build the institutional form of the church. The church is a means, not an end. Yet an adequate institutional form is necessary if there is to be adequate means for people to be served by the church and also to serve through it. A congregation at worship is receiving and being served. The congregation at work in the community is transmitting and is serving. The lines of communication are Christian people in their daily lives.

To live a Christian way of life in a changing community constitutes the transmission of the message to people in the actual situation of their lives. A congregation is a community called by God to communicate the call to faith to people in the larger human society. The extent to which members of a congregation think, speak and act out of Christian concern and love determines the degree to which the message is communicated.

The individual Christian's way of life reflects his orientation to life and his beliefs and values. How he conducts himself in relation to others is his witness. When his way of life is in accord with the message, he shares and witnesses as God intends. But is communication so subtle as to be bound up with the way one lives? Yes, it is just this plain and evident. Public obedience to the Christian message is communication. The Word becomes flesh and lives among men.

As servant of the congregation, the pastor's service is to be a spokesman of the message. To fulfill his office he must know the Christian message in depth, he is a servant of the Word. The pastor must love his congregation and live its life. Observation of the struggles of people in changing communities is not enough. It takes the experiences of participation in the struggle to equip a man to be a spokesman.

As a congregation exists to build people and not the reverse, so, too, the reason for the existence of auxiliary organizations of a congregation is to build and serve people. People are not meant to be used to build these organizations. They are not ends in themselves. They are meant to be the means for serving people. Careful consideration needs to be given by a congregation to see to it that its auxiliary organizations contribute to the communication of the Christian message and help demonstrate a way of life.

Obstacles in Communication

The church tends to concentrate on redemption and to have a minimal concern for creation. To limit communication of the Christian message to only a part of it constitutes an obstacle. Creation is basic. God's first act is creation. People live in creation and they are part of it. They work in communities and on farms and deal constantly with creation. What has God to say to man about his creation? Perhaps the church has not sufficiently recognized this significance. The impact of modern technology tends to place God in the background. He is used to explain the unknown and is not seen in what is known. The phenomena with which agricultural technology works illustrate the orderliness by which God operates creation. "The mystery of electricity and the ecology of the micro-organisms of the soil both contribute in a special way to agricultural production. But both are governed by God."[1] A timid, withdrawn understanding of creation is no trumpet for communicating the Christian message. An underdeveloped doctrine of creation meekly applied to life sounds a flat note in the ear of the county agent, farmer, grain elevator manager and small town mayor.

The mere verbalizing of words, phrases or ideas, tends to be equated with the communication of the Christian message. Caught up in the developments and vocabulary of the agricultural and technological revolutions, man no longer understands the church's old terms. The communication of a congregation which counts is that of relating the Christian message to people. When the message is reduced to a repetition of pious words or phrases the communication of the Christian message is reduced accordingly.

The all-important task of the church in changing town and country communities is to communicate the Christian message, but this tends to become diffused in the institutional functions of congregations. Typical comments of church members bear this out. "The Johnson family ought to belong to our church. They would make good members." Building membership for its own sake takes place at the expense of sharing the Christian message. To do the right thing for the wrong reason sacrifices basic values and ultimately contributes to decadence rather than strength.

Church people sometimes become involved in social need because of the need itself. Christian motivation does not lie in needs but elsewhere. When a social need becomes the reason for service the communication of the Christian message suffers. Christian motivation is rooted in Christ. He sends the Christian to serve in the changing world. The needs of people in changing communities are the occasion for Christian concern and involvement but not the reason.

Attitudes of church people can be obstacles to communication. Church members suffer economic reverses and experience social reverses as do non-members. Sometimes laymen or pastors become apathetic or pessimistic because of such reverses. But when attitudes of indifference or hopelessness characterize a person he no longer has a message.

FOOTNOTE

[1]*The Church and Agricultural Progress*, United States Department of Agriculture, May 1962, page 5.

13.

RELATING RESPONSIBLY
TO AGRICULTURE

Agriculture is a complex interrelated industry which is difficult to understand. The notion which many churchmen hold of farming and the entire agricultural enterprise tends to be outdated and oversimplified. "Farming employs 7.4 million workers —more than the combined employment in transportation, public utilities, the steel industry, and the automobile industry."[1] It is imperative for the church to relate responsibly to the economic and social factors in agriculture and rural life.

Leaders Need to Know

The success of American agriculture in developing a sustained increase in the capacity to produce has paradoxically brought about the farm problems of over-supply and the relative decline of farm prices. Success in the technology of production is not matched in the area of distribution, marketing or supply management. Inadequate income for farmers and the decreasing occupational opportunities in farming, which contribute to unemployment, are serious economic and social problems which demand attention by the responsible elements of our society. Since the church desires to relate to all sectors of American society it must also be concerned with economic and social problems related to agriculture.

Ethical and moral decisions are always involved in economic and social change. What are the responsibilities of all the various members of rural society in the current farm crisis? What are the guides for ethical action in production control, collective bargaining, free markets and "sharing our surplus" as means to bring about a closer balance between supply and demand? What are the marks of a responsible farm organization? The church can help to study and to state ethical and moral guidelines which will assist persons to deal responsibly with the farm crisis and the rapid changes in town and country society. For churchmen to deal with these concerns responsibly it is necessary that they be familiar with agriculture and rural life.

Confronted by the reality of inadequate income, farmers have made and are making various decisions: increasing the efficiency and size of their farm operations in order to obtain an adequate income; taking part-time employment to bolster the family income; cutting back the farm operation in order to hold down gross costs; leaving farming altogether in favor of other employment in small town or urban business and industry. Rapid technological change has also left a backlog of American farmers who, for one reason or another, have been unable to adapt and adjust to the new technology. Each of these different causes carries with it implications not only for the farmer but also for town and country communities—their businesses, their schools and, not the least, their churches.

People who remain in farming and increase the size of their operation are confronted by the need for capital. In view of the returns, how large an indebtedness can safely be taken on? Where off-the-farm employment occurs, adjustments in family patterns and work loads are necessary. Cutting back the size of farm operations to reduce costs brings with it less potential income. The well-being of farmers who do not adapt or adjust to the changing farm technology is threatened. In each of these general situations severe economic and social tensions may develop. The farmer needs to be seen as a person faced with the problems of farming.

People who leave farming for employment in towns and cities also have adjustments to make. The uprooting of a family from its farm in order to move to the city can be a very severe experience. Farm youth who decide not to go into farming are confronted with the problem of financing a college education or other special training.

Farm organizations hold opposing positions as to the solution of the farm problem. In a given community or congregation the farmers themselves join different farm organizations with conflicting positions. The positions and the solutions of the organizations are often supported with a high degree of emotion by its members. Sometimes a community and a congregation become seriously divided over the issues.

Political parties also sponsor different solutions to farm problems. As in the case of farm organizations, these solutions may be held with considerable emotion by local people and they can cause tensions in the community or in the congregation.

National View Important

Church leaders have a responsibility to become familiar with agriculture as a national industry. They also need to be acquainted with the types of agriculture and farm operations engaged in locally and in the region and with current developments and problems. Sometimes church leaders evaluate the farm problem only from the point of view of the consumer, or the taxpayer. Church leaders need to see farm problems from the farmer's point of view as well. When church leaders display a resentment toward a particular agricultural program or offer oversimplified solutions to the farm problem, farmers are chagrined. When church leaders display a keen interest in farming and farm problems and are willing to learn more from persons who are informed, farmers are encouraged.

Agencies, boards and divisions of church bodies which serve on a regional or national basis are duty bound to become familiar with the entire constituency they serve. In our increasingly urban society program planning tends to be designed with urban society in mind. Offices are most often located in a large city.

Staff members live in the city. Urban contacts in church and secular affairs are more frequent than contacts with agriculture and rural life. Our communication, transportation and residential patterns make it advisable to locate service units of the church in large population centers. Personal contacts and mass communication may unnoticingly over-influence church leaders and staff people unless they make a deliberate effort to become familiar with the agricultural industry and with town and country society.

A recent study of the U. S. Department of Labor indicates that farmers have the longest average work week of any occupation in the country. (The second highest average number of hours per week was that of managers in business and industry.) Another study showed that the average annual income of farmers is at the lowest end of the scale. Evangelism, parish education and stewardship agencies, for example, need to be aware of such information as they plan programs for their constituencies. Farmers, in general, have less real income to share with the church and fewer hours to devote to its programs. This does not mean that farmers are less willing to give to or to work for their church. But it does mean that church leaders and church agencies need to be aware of the social and economic factors which affect farmers and people living in farm communities. They may make up a very large part, and, in some instances, a majority of the constituents served.

Appreciation and understanding of the scope and importance of agriculture and rural life can help to strengthen the American society as a whole. The United States has the most diverse and productive agriculture in the world. It also has highly developed communications and transportation systems. But there is insufficient communication and understanding between rural and urban people. A lack of communication between the farm and city contributes to divisiveness, self-interest and tension. Constructive action calls for increased communication and mutual appreciation.

Many church bodies had their beginnings close to the land.

A majority of their members were farmers and people who worked in farm-related occupations. Congregations were established and grew in many small communities. Church leadership was quite directly related to agriculture and rural life. Many church bodies continue to have large constituencies in rural areas, many of which are increasing in numbers. Church bodies are now confronted by the agricultural revolution and the emerging structure of town and country society. The study of agriculture and small communities is important for church leadership in the changing situation.

The size of the population in rural areas of the United States is not generally given adequate attention. Unending publicity about the twin trends of urbanization and the decline of the number of farms tend to obscure the size of the rural population. Long-range trends are more significant than those of short periods of time. In 1900 there were 46 million people classified as "rural" in the U. S. according to census findings. By 1960 it was 54 million. The number of people in rural areas has not diminished. Rather it has increased. Rural nonfarm residents are adding new thousands in many town and country areas.[2] The characteristics of agriculture, rural communities and social patterns have altered as the country has shifted from a predominantly agricultural to a predominantly industrial society. The size of the rural population, changes affecting it, and its growth, merit serious attention by church leaders.

What Can Be Done Locally

Serious study of agriculture and rural life can be constructive for pastors serving in town and country areas. People living on farms or in small towns develop greater respect for the clergy if the clergy show a genuine interest in their work. Agricultural developments, farm practices, the objectives and programs of farm organizations, and also community development offer the perceptive pastor ample opportunity for observation and study. Pastors who have an interest in these areas find that parishioners seek them out to listen and "to talk things over." Encouragement to a parishioner by a pastor can be of significant help.

Different solutions to farm problems, or issues in a community, sometimes split people in the community into strongly opposing groups. This can happen within a congregation as well. During the recent National Farmers Organization action of holding livestock on the farm in an attempt to raise prices, it was reported that some congregations "were split down the middle." The pastor who has a knowledge of farm problems, and who has avoided the pitfall of taking sides, is in a position to help people become reconciled when enmities develop. He can help people with strongly held viewpoints to agree to disagree and yet respect one another in a Christian manner.

Adult and youth auxiliary organizations in the congregation provide an opportunity for discussing issues in farming and in the agricultural industry. Persons in auxiliary organizations frequently represent a cross-section of occupations in the community, including farming, while community organizations sometimes have only special interest groups. Informative discussions among laymen and the pastor in church organizations offer opportunities for strengthening the concern and understanding of the church for agriculture and rural life.

There are two basic ways in which the layman can assist his pastor to learn the problems of agriculture and rural life. First, he can help his pastor to understand the current situation locally. To do this he may share informative articles in farm magazines, take his pastor to visit farms and invite him to meetings where leaders discuss problems and developments in agriculture. Second, the layman can help the pastor identify farm families who are experiencing financial and social difficulties. The layman and the pastor can work together to help such families through personal contact and by encouraging the family to call on economic and social agencies which have the appropriate services for assistance and information.

On the local scene the layman is obligated to participate in a farm organization of his choice. As a member of a farm organization he can help it to function responsibly. It is to be expected that people and organizations will differ as to what method and practices are best suited to current farm issues and how best to improve the farmer's income. But these differences must not be permitted to divide congregations or communities. While the layman may legitimately oppose what his neighbor or his neighbor's organization recommends he ought never allow this to cause him to take a negative attitude toward his neighbor as a person. The farm income crisis demands all church people to be considerate and objective and to exert a reconciling influence to counterbalance some of the necessary tensions that are generated.

FOOTNOTES

[1]*Background on Our Nation's Agriculture*, United States Department of Agriculture, Office of Information, Leaflet No. 491.

[2]For a report on the growing nonfarm population see *New Thousands in Town and Country, Concern of the Church*, National Lutheran Council, Division of American Missions, 327 South LaSalle St., Chicago 4, Illinois, 1962, 127 pages.

14.

THE INDIVIDUAL AND
A MEANINGFUL LIFE

"What satisfaction is there in farming when year after year there are surpluses and nobody appreciates what we're doing? And when higher costs keep shrinking your income?" Such statements are being made or thought by countless farmers in the changing rural society. A key word in the statement is satisfaction. Involved in the individual farmer's meaning of the word is his feeling of personal worth and the purpose of his work.

A farm implement franchise is bought and moved from a small community, ending the employment of its two employees. In rural communities, forces beyond control of the individual affect his economic and social patterns. Sooner or later his thoughts of the meaning of life are affected too.

Picture Hometown in June. Some of its young people return from colleges and universities. One of them, named Douglas, has just completed his sophomore year at the land-grant university. He wants to become an agricultural statistician but wonders whether his parents approve. The college group gets together in familiar places but Randy feels embarrassed around them. He has just finished a six-week course to become a heavy equipment operator. Jim sees his former classmates around town but avoids talking to them. Since graduation he has not found a steady job and he feels he can not leave home. Three young men in the changing rural environment—they and their peers seek a meaningful life.

Newtonville, USA, is a growing town 33 miles from the state capitol. New houses are going up in every neighborhood. They call it a bedroom town but it is hard to find a place to park on the main street. Over on the north side is a new retirement home. It can accommodate 175 people and it's full. Its residents ponder life's meaning.

In a mid-America town a businessman ran his lumberyard capably while his children were at home. When they left the quality of service and inventory became a disappointment in the community. The local medical doctor is caught in the swirl of overwork but he is unyielding in his opposition toward community efforts to secure another physician. Both the businessman and the doctor are less than inspiring in their attitude toward life.

The particular situations in which individuals seek a meaningful life are as numerous as the persons who live in rural society. Brief descriptions can not typify individuals for no two circumstances are alike. However, the problem of finding a meaningful life in rural society has some common elements.

Some Factors in the Problem

Many people in the changing rural society may not have an adequate foundation for a meaningful life. The individual's adjustment to change and the character of his social relationships are dependent upon his motivation. In many individuals a recognition of divine call may be insufficiently established or altogether absent. There may be little or no appreciation of the Christian meaning of service to one's neighbor. A meaningful life requires a cause for which to live and work.

Individuals and communities in mid-America sometimes settle for goals which are beneath their capacity. Farming, business, local government, schools and community life negatively influence the individual when they lapse into mediocrity, and this in turn contributes to the loss of a needed sense of achievement. Standards of excellence are necessary in mid-America communities as a positive environment for the individual to develop his potential and for the discovery of meaning in performance.

Rural people sometimes betray the lack of meaning in rural life by an overemphasis on negative aspects. "Farming is just a gamble." "Blink when you drive through our town and you'll miss it." "Hometown isn't what it used to be." There is a need for rural people to view life in a positive sense. In farming, as in all occupations, the element of risk is present, but it is a calculated risk. Small communities can be significant places in which to live and work, in spite of change, provided the people are willing to give them significance through their best efforts.

For many decades rural society has been a refuge for independent thought and action. In the less complex economy of former years the farmer prized his freedom in making choices and decisions. With the development of national agricultural policies and programs and the development of the mass market, the pressure to conform to larger patterns have lessened his independence, but he continues to prize it. The competition which he meets today is found in larger elements and they are more remote. The rural worker also had more freedom of movement. If he did not like his job he could rather easily qualify for another. To qualify for another job today he needs retraining. For a meaningful life personal decision making is an important process.

While rapid social change in rural society has made the discovery of a meaningful life difficult, the church in some ways has contributed to the problem. At times it has been irrelevant. In instances, divisive. It tends to conform to secular values. The congregation may show great interest in getting the newly arrived school principal and his family into membership, but there may be 100 or more families in the area or county (of a low income level) whose lives have not been touched by "the communion of saints." The criterion for its program may not be so much the Gospel of St. John as St. John's, the congregation on the other side of town. Rural society needs congregations which have a message that is related to the situation, which contributes a unifying influence in the community, and which demonstrates a concern for all people.

Sources of Help

What can be done to help the individual to find a meaningful life in the changing rural society? Through its faith the church must make a contribution to the individual.

The Christian church affirms its faith in God and the purpose he intends for man. Through his acts of creation and redemption, God gives man the possibility for a meaningful life. The individual is to find meaning in coming to know God and in serving his fellowman for God's sake.

The farmer or rural community employee may experience considerable difficulty in adjusting to the changing economic and social situations in which he finds himself. Yet this is precisely the situation in which the individual is called to give his allegiance to God and to give his finest service to his fellowman.

The Christian answer to meaning in life in the changing rural society is not an easy answer. It recognizes conflicts and upsetting circumstances. But life is a struggle and a life to be full must engage in the struggle. Both the Old and the New Testaments portray dramatic accounts of struggle in life and contain admonitions to engage in it. In the biblical accounts, individuals who yield their allegiance to God and serve their fellowman are those whose lives have meaning. Those who give up the struggle or settle for lesser goals than God intends lose life's meaning.

God is active in bringing about his purpose and meaning through the life of the individual. He places man where he wants him to be, putting spiritual and material resources at the disposal of man. God gives the essentials and man is to develop them.

The church can help individuals find meaning in life by extending encouragement and fellowship. No one can find a meaningful life in isolation. The church is to provide the individual both the certainty of belonging and the opportunities for service to others.

Rural youth have a sense of isolation when their aspirations and problems are neglected. Young people concerned for their future are in need of what the church can give them. As the church extends them encouragement and fellowship they will be aided in their struggle for meaning. A pastor or layman can help a youth through personal conversation as well as through church youth programs. In both approaches, ideas involved in the Christian understanding of vocation can be shared to help our youth discover meaning in the midst of struggle.

Elderly people in the rural society need the fellowship of the church. A ministry to them is a responsibility of the pastor. Immeasurable help to countless retired persons is given through pastoral visits. But persons in their senior years can also find joy and fulfillment when youth and adult laymen of the church call on them. Where these visits take place both the visited and the visitor frequently bear witness of the spontaneous joy and meaning which accrue. However, untold thousands of older people in rural communities live in relative isolation and yearn for the discovery or rediscovery of meaning.

A rural community has the potential to help the individual find a meaningful life. How can this be accomplished? One of the ways is through the development of a concern for individual residents by the community. When a community demonstrates a concern for an individual he experiences a sense of being united with it, and thus is more likely to have a greater sense of responsibility to it. In this interaction the individual grows in his social relationships and this can help him develop a meaningful life.

Rural community development is another way by which a community may help the individual find a meaningful life. Community development can provide an environment with standards and goals conducive to response by the individual. Leaders can coordinate their efforts through a community or area committee to encourage and assist the improvement of community appearance, businesses, government, employment opportunities, schools and other services. When a businessman, who has allowed the quality of his service to fall, is confronted by general community improvements he is more likely to set new goals for himself. Achievement of individual and community goals can yield meaning in life for the individual. Members of the community committee may help the individual to find meaning by a recognition of the contribution he makes to the community and by expressions of encouragement and appreciation.

Professional services in the rural community are important for the individual. Where there are unfulfilled needs or where a professional person has more work than he can competently take care of, the community leaders should take the initiative to secure the needed personnel. The professional person who resists help in the same profession may discover that no one, himself included, is indispensable. What may first be interpreted as interference may ultimately come to be regarded as community service and result in a more meaningful life for the professional person. Adequate professional services in the community are important supports to the individual residents.

The Need to Look Ahead

To help the individual to find a meaningful life in the changing rural society, the basic economic and social realities need to be identified and accepted. In rural society there tends to be a desire to wait for the return of things as they used to be, and there is a pressing need for people and communities to take a studied look at the future.

Change is not new to American rural society. Since the earliest mechanical inventions in farming, American agriculture has pioneered the research and development which has wrought economic and social change. Innovations in animal husbandry, chemical processes of fertilizers and sprays, new sources of financial credit, plant genetics, mass marketing and other innovations have spawned the agricultural revolution. And new methods of agriculture have not ceased. Research and experimentation are developing new ways and processes which will continue to bring change at an even more rapid rate.

While change can not be forestalled it can be guided. While change does not leave people unaffected, steps can be taken to adjust to it so that it can be constructive rather than harmful.

Change itself may unfold new opportunities and new responsibilities. Automation has released millions of Americans from tedious work and has resulted in the rapid growth of recreation and vacation time. Recreation is now one of the fastest growing large industries in the country.

Automation on the farm has made it possible for one farmer to supply enough food for 27 persons whereas formerly he could supply only five. Intensive farming practices today require fewer acres than in the past. Recreation is a major economic opportunity and social responsibility in rural areas.

The development of a river system or watershed in a geographical region may remove thousands of acres from direct farm use but may result in supporting expanded economic activity, a larger population and new forms of agriculture in the region.

The individual needs assistance and information to see and to take advantage of imminent opportunities. When rural people look ahead and prepare themselves for the economic and social structures which are emerging they are in the best position to help guide change, to accept new opportunities and to develop a meaningful life.

In addition to the spiritual counsel a pastor shares with the members of his congregation, he may encourage the individual to inventory his personal aptitudes and capabilities. Encouragement can be given by a pastor to adjust to changes and to take advantage of new occupations and areas of service. The interest which a pastor takes in looking ahead can help individuals in the congregation and community.

The changes occurring in rural society point to the need for recognizing the larger areas of economic and social functions. A pastor can encourage the people of his community to relate to the larger emerging area. Narrow loyalty to a specific community may do more harm than be helpful. For example, reluctance to develop a parish or a school in a geographical area larger than one small town may deprive children in the area of sufficient resources for a program that fills their needs.

The future of individual and community is dependent upon their character, beliefs and attitudes. People need to develop all their capacities so that they can deal with change basically through their own efforts and so that they can achieve a meaningful life.

15.

CHRISTIAN GOALS
FOR THE FAMILY

Despite the advancements that have occurred in all other areas of life there is a persisting tendency to picture the farm of today as it was fifty years ago. This romantic, somewhat sentimental view of the farm is sometimes pictured in movies and television. It is a happy, uncomplicated life, virtually unaffected by the changes of the 20th century. And most important to this discussion, the farm is generally accorded to be the ideal place for a family. The farm is considered a family enterprise and the family itself a tightly-knit unit, and because of its common tasks and purpose, the farm family is thought to achieve a closeness no other can possess. That this picture is based on nostalgia and not reality can become starkly apparent if one chooses to look.

Today the family in mid-America is caught up by and involved in automation and technology. Radical change is all about. In the 1960's the family in mid-America, on the farms and in the small communities, is not what it was in the first half of the century, and not even what is was in the 50's. The old image is obsolete and unreal. Mobility is characteristic of people in small communities. Their occupations are specialized. Farmers work with the newest products of such technologies as chemistry, engineering, finance, marketing, plant biophysics and animal genetics.

The changes which have affected the farms and communities in mid-America have not left families unaffected. What influences have been at work? What are some characteristics of the family today? What are Christian goals and purposes for the family? How can the church help the family to achieve true Christian goals and purposes?

Influences Affecting the Family

The achievement of the goal of high agricultural production is a development which influences the family in mid-America. The transition from a primarily agricultural and rural society to a primarily industrial and urban society is based on the accomplishment of that goal. With the new agricultural technologies, economic and social structures have come into being. It is essential that the church recognize the economic and social forces which are exerting profound influences on the family.

Economic functions by the family as a unit have been greatly reduced. The number of people now living on family farms is a small fraction of the entire population. The family grocery store is the exception rather than the rule. Where there are family-owned businesses and shops, employees rather than family members supply most of the labor. The economic ties which bound families together in interdependence no longer exist as they once did.

Parents spend less time in the family. More fathers in mid-America work away from the home than ever before. Earning the family's breadwinning income lessens contact with the family. More mothers in mid-America are engaged in economic duties away from home. Modern household conveniences and childbearing during earlier years of life are changing homemaking from a full-time occupation, to a part-time occupation. Women are more free to accept employment away from the home. And they do.

Speaking in economic terms, children in the families of today are no longer "assets." Rather they are "liabilities." Their needs and wants exceed that which they can contribute in work and service to the family unit. As children complete high school

economic dependence while in college or trade school frequently continues.

Grandparents are separated from the family and exert less
influence than in former generations. They may or may not
have adequate provisions for retirement. But they seldom live
with their family. There is no place for them in the homes of
their relatives. They have social security and retirement homes.

The rural family is now less a producing unit and is more
a buying and consuming unit. This is true both for the necessities of life and the luxuries. Between old rural values and
those now guiding most rural families there is a struggle. Thrift,
saving and self-denial largely have given way to spending, use
of credit and the possession of material goods. Parents want
and buy the appliances and appointments available for the
home, and advertising excites the appetites of teenagers for
many things.

More teenage marriages as well as many ill-prepared for and
unwise marriages are occurring in mid-America. Changes in
dating and courtship practices and more opportunity for economic employment for young people are some contributing factors. Earlier marriage is an influence on the family.

Some Characteristics of the Family Today

Family instability characterizes a greater number of families
in mid-America today. Family members have less activity and
time together with the reduction of family economic functions.
Solidarity based on a family economic enterprise is diminished
and it is not likely to return. Many families have not found
common bonds sufficiently strong to replace the influence of
the common economic enterprise.

Parental direction and control is lessening its hold on the
family. The simple fact of the father working away from home
lessens his immediate influence. (This does not mean that the
quality of the paternal influence necessarily is jeopardized.) The
father may be forfeiting an undue degree of paternal influence

by transferring it to the mother or to an older child. The influence of gainful employment away from the home by women
tends to result in less influence by the mother. When children
are left in the care of others, and placed in day nurseries or
left to shift for themselves, the child's need for his parent tends
to be met less adequately. While the family is not together nearly as much as it once was, it does have more income.

Children and grandparents are affected by other new economic and social patterns. When there is no productive work
or chores to be done by children, they may be left without
any way in which to contribute to the family. When grandparents live apart from their relatives, children do not have
the opportunity to come to know their grandparents as intimately as they once did. The influence of grandparents may be
positive or negative, but in either case, when grandparents are
not present neither the whole family nor the children have the
influence of the older generation. (Some of the finest learning
experiences of children in the past, in their development of attitudes and interests, are the occasions when they were taught
by grandparents in the home. Parents may not have, or may
not take, the time to teach children. Grandparents generally
have the time and the desire to teach.)

The incidence of broken homes and divorces increases with
the rise in the numbers of teenage and ill-prepared-for marriages, and with the increase of the numbers of either or both
husband and wife who work away from the family unit. While
the number and proportion of broken homes and divorces climbs,
the number of marriages is climbing more sharply. More parents are remarried divorcees and more children live in families
characterized by remarriage. Before the turn of the century only
one marriage out of 500 ended in divorce as compared with
the present one out of four. Another result is the increased
incidence of "families" in which children live with a single
divorced parent.

A greater dependence on units in society other than the family is resulting from the decrease in economic enterprise by

the family as a unit. There is a greater dependence on school, church and community organizations. While parents, too, need the family for stabilizing the adult personality, the demands of work and adult social organizations tends to deprive parents of the family time they need. The family role in meeting the needs of both children and adults is being reduced.

Christian Goals and Purposes

In the beginning God created man and woman. He ordained marriage and the family. The family was created to be a social and religious unit. God intended that each member of the family obey him and have a living relationship to him. The central Christian goal and purpose for the family today is that all members of the family obey God and have a living relationship to him.

Several supporting goals within the family need to be mentioned. The family needs stability, wholeness and permanence. These are based on the stability, wholesomeness and permanence of marriage. An enduring marriage is both built by the individual and contributes to the individual. The development of the individual's ability and readiness to contribute to the other is essential. To exploit or to neglect the other party in marriage in a self-centered manner contributes to family instability and dissolution.

Children need to be able to be constructive participants in the family. The sense of being and gratification which results from contributing to the family is not confined to adults. The spontaneity of the creative urge of children to do things for the family, however child-like these may be, is the very fiber of that human quality which God gives to man. The encouragement and guidance of children in their contributions to the family is a helpful supporting goal.

In the beginning man was given a responsibility to conduct himself in human relationships in a God-pleasing manner. These relationships exist within and among families. Each member of the family is to participate in the larger community in a manner which reflects God's way with man. Each member of the family can help in the development of the community of families.

Responsibility for the categories of creation, "every living thing," was also given to man. A purpose of the family, therefore, is to exercise care for creation—animals, micro-organisms of the soil, plants and water.

For such purposes did God create families on farms and in the communities of mid-America today. Economic, technological and social changes do not alter the goals and purposes for the family. They merely change the culture—the forms and shapes of things within creation. In each culture the family is to achieve goals and fulfill its purposes.

How the Church Can Help

Before a congregation can help the family to achieve Christian goals and purposes it is necessary that the congregation examine its own goals and purposes. A congregation is not ready to assist families until it recognizes the importance of the family unit and is committed to a ministry to the family, and understands the characteristics of the families it seeks to minister to, and prepares itself for a ministry to the family. A congregation, like other social institutions, tends to conduct its service to people as individuals. This is easier and less complicated, but less effective.

The first task of the congregation in helping the family is to be a church to the family. As the instrument of God for the process of reconciliation the church has a message. The full communication of that message is the service God intends the congregation to render to the family.

Study of the Christian concepts of marriage and the family is basic in a congregation. In re-evaluating them, traditional ideas and practice may be challenged. Unresolved issues may be discovered. Emotional and intellectual tensions may arise.

The goal of a relevant ministry to the family makes the examination worthwhile, whatever the risks. As the concepts of Christian marriage and family are re-evaluated in the congregation by each successive generation, contemporary family life will be emotionally, intellectually and spiritually more rich and vital. Furthermore, there is no realistic alternative to gain an understanding of Christian marriage and the family which is adequate for modern times.

The community is important for the congregation in its ministry to families. Influences affecting families vary from community to community. So do the characteristics of families. No two communities or families are precisely the same. Social scientists draw information and conclusions from data which is broadly based. Such information is helpful. But the congregation will do well to know the influences and characteristics for the families within its own community and area. Specific information can be gathered by a congregation with the assistance of social scientists and by using the methods of social science.

The congregation has a responsibility to identify Christian goals and purposes for the families it seeks to serve. Many American families possess only a vague understanding of them and only a wavering commitment to them. As the goals and purposes are identified by people and pastor together, communication has begun. As the people develop a clearer understanding of the goals and purposes for the family, a firmer commitment is made possible. With commitment comes a way of life. And a way of life can and does communicate to the community.

Adequate qualifications and preparation for marriage and family life can be encouraged by the congregation. Unstable marriages and families reflect deficient qualifications and/or preparation. Individuals may lack the character and spiritual commitment to establish a Christian marriage and family. In such cases help for the individual toward becoming a whole person may be the most beneficial service to render. Preparation for a wholesome marriage begins in wholesome family life. The teaching and counseling service of the congregation can be of great help in preparing people for marriage and family life.

A congregation, or group of congregations in rural areas, may explore and develop approaches in helping the family to achieve Christian goals. Conferences or institutes on dating, courtship, the family and making of a home may be sponsored. These may include information to parents to help them to prepare their children for responsible adult life and marriage. Libraries which include books on subject areas related to the family are an invaluable resource a congregation can offer. Congregations may also share information about public or   private agencies and institutions which have programs to serve the family. Young adults, being fewer in number than any other age group in small towns and rural areas, tend to be the least served. Together within the community, congregations may be able to to meet the diverse interests and needs of young adults.

There is a need for a congregation to structure its programs in ways which will encourage the family to participate as a family. This approach has possibilities in parish education, worship, auxiliary organizations, recreational activities and work projects. The cultivation of family-centered events of the church can help to develop a more wholesome life within families. A congregation may also contribute to family life by showing a concern for and an interest in the participation of individuals in community responsibilities.

Some thought needs to be given to the family-like functions of a congregation to people, especially to unmarried men and women, widows, widowers, and divorcees. It is not without good reason that the term family is frequently applied to the church. To worship and have fellowship with the family of God can meet a human need for family. A congregation does well to consider the family-like meanings which can and ought to accrue to people in its worship and fellowship. In mid-America communities the numerous single persons as well as married persons and children can have a more meaningful life in congregations which recognize and help meet the human desire and need for family.

AFTERWORD
THE CHURCH—A DECISIVE FACTOR

The church has received its message from the Lord; it can look to no other source. Through contemplation, study, prayer, and the guidance of the Holy Spirit, the church seeks to understand more fully the divine truth the Lord has entrusted to it.

However, it is not enough to understand the message. The assignment that the Lord gave to the church means that it is to communicate the truth. The writers of the Gospels and the Epistles understood the historical social setting of the people to whom they addressed their writings. This was essential if they were to communicate their message.

What Is the Social Situation?

The church is hindered in the communication of its message if it does not understand the historical and socio-economic situations of the people to whom it is speaking. It is not enough that a few of its scholars know this. It is essential that the pastor and the lay leaders know the social situation of the people to whom their congregation is called to minister.

The church has many programs, such as stewardship, evangelism, and education. The designers of these programs need to be familiar with the socio-economic situation of the congregations for whom they are designing these programs. The designer of farm equipment is familiar with the climate and the terrain on which the farm equipment will be used. In the same way

161

the designers of church programs must be familiar with the socio-economic climate of the communities in which congregations will be putting to use the programs they design.

It is not necessary that each program make its own study of the social situation. Stewardship of time and effort suggests that the different church bodies and the designers of different church programs ask that objective studies be made periodically of the social situation in which the people to whom the church must communicate the Gospel work and live. Furthermore, the results of these studies need to be compiled so that they have immediate and practical value to laymen, pastors, and administrators.

Mid-America Is a Key Area

In mid-America the ratio of church membership to population is high. There is a significant number of church-owned or church-directed educational institutions. The church supplies many social services. Many congregations are being served by qualified pastors. A good working relationship exists between the church and state educational resources. Outdoor recreation is available to all its citizens.

Mid-America is a geographical area that has been blessed with a rich soil and with many other natural resources. It has a thriving agriculture, built on many well-developed family farms. It has many villages and medium-sized cities which serve as business service centers. It has a number of industrial centers and a few large metropolitan centers. At present there is a balance between farming and manufacturing. But its main resource is its people.

The Future Is in Question

Yet all is not well in the heartland of our country. Forces which represent self-centered interests move more aggressively than the forces which represent community interests. It is a new experience for many to work together in the interest of developing quality communities. The past for some is a pleasant memory. The future, because of the many changes and necessary adjustments, is faced with anxiety. Conflicting forces compete for the loyalty of the people. The meaning of life has become hazy for many.

The six issues identified and discussed at the workshop indicate areas of concern to which the church must give attention. Mid-America is ripe for creative leadership. The church can supply this leadership:

If it concretely and fully articulates the Christian message;

If it is conversant with the socio-economic situations of mid-America;

If it can challenge and guide the congregations to put their own parish organizations in order and relate their ministry to the local community;

If it thinks in terms of definite goals for mid-America;

If it knows how to marshall its own resources;

If it understands and assists community development;

If it has the capacity to relate itself to the total Christian enterprise.

At this point it is not certain whether the church has the desire and the will to provide leadership in all these areas. There is doubt as to what forces will win in the silent struggle for mid-America.

SELECTED BIBLIOGRAPHY

Agriculture and Rural Life

Buck, Pearl S., *The Townsman.* New York: The John Day Company, 1961.

Christian, C. F., ed., *Adjustments in Agriculture—a National Basebook.* Ames, Iowa: Iowa State University Press, 1961.

Davis, John, and Hinshaw, Kenneth, *Farmer in a Business Suit.* New York: Simon and Schuster, 1957.

Higbee, Edward, *Farms and Farmers in an Urban Age.* New York: The Twentieth Century Fund, 1963.

Hitch, Earle, *Rebuilding Rural America.* New York: Harper and Brothers Publishers, 1950.

Hudson, Lois Phillips, *The Bones of Plenty.* Boston: Little Brown and Company, 1962.

Keener, Orrin L., *Struggle for Equal Opportunity.* New York: Vantage Press, 1961.

Stefferud, Alfred, editor, *After a Hundred Years, the Yearbook of Agriculture 1962.* Washington, D.C.: U.S. Government Printing Office, 1962.

Stefferud, Alfred, editor, *Power to Produce.* Washington, D.C.: U.S. Government Printing Office, 1960.

Tossett, Otis, *Land, Water and People.* St. Paul, Minnesota: Webb Publishing Company, 1961.

————, *Goals and Values in Agricultural Policy.* Ames, Iowa: Iowa State University Press, 1961.

————, *Report on the Commission on Country Life.* Chapel Hill, North Carolina: University of North Carolina Press, 1944.

————, *Continuing Education and Country Life.* Chicago: American Country Life Association, 1961.

————, *Our Town and Country Society Looks at Itself.* Chicago: American Country Life Association, 1962.

Church in Town and Country

Bockelman, Wilfred, *On Good Soil*. New York: Friendship Press, 1959.

Carr, James McLeod, *Our Church Meeting Human Needs*. Birmingham, Alabama: The Progressive Farmer Company, 1962.

Cleveland, Philip J., *It's Bright in My Valley*. Westwood, New Jersey: F. H. Revell Company, 1962.

DeVries, Charles, *Inside Rural America: A Lutheran View*. Chicago: National Lutheran Council, 1962.

Gullixson, T. F., *In the Face of the West Wind*. Minneapolis. Augsburg Publishing House, 1963.

Greene, Shirley E., *Frement on the Fringe*. Philadelphia: The Christian Education Press, 1960.

McBride, C. R., *Protestant Churchmanship for Rural America*. Valley Forge, Pennsylvania: Judson Press, 1962.

Mueller, E. W., and Skold, Betty Westrom, *Pastor, How Can You Expect . . .* Chicago: National Lutheran Council, 1960.

Mueller, E. W., *Stewardship of the Countryside*. Chicago: National Lutheran Council, 1963.

Obenhaus, Victor, *The Church and Faith in Mid-America*. Philadelphia: The Westminster Press, 1963.

Randolph, Henry S., and Patton, Betty Jean, *Orientation to the Town and Country Church*. New York: The United Presbyterian Church in the U.S.A., 1961.

Richter, Conrad, *A Simple Honorable Man*. New York: Alfred A. Knopf, 1962.

Smith, Rockwell C., *People, Land, and Churches*. New York: Friendship Press, 1959.

————, *New Thousands in Town and Country, Concern of the Church*. Chicago: Church in Town and Country, National Lutheran Council, 1962.

Sociology and Economics

Bogue, Donald J., and Beale, Calvin L., *Economic Areas of the United States*. New York: Free Press of Glencoe, 1961.

Galbraith, John Kenneth, *The Affluent Society*. Cambridge, Massachusetts: The Riverside Press, 1958.

Hoiberg, Otto, *Exploring the Small Community*. Lincoln, Nebraska: University of Nebraska Press, 1955.

Kreitlow, Burton W., *Rural Education: Community Backgrounds*. New York: Harper and Brothers Publishers, 1954.

Kreitlow, Burton W., Aiton, E. W., and Torrence, Andrew P., *Leadership for Action in Rural Communities*. Danville, Illinois: The Interstate Printers and Publishers, Inc., 1960.

Lionberger, H. F., *Adoption of New Ideas and Practices*. Ames, Iowa: Iowa State University Press, 1960.

Nelson, Lowry, *The Minnesota Community: Country and Town in Transition*. Minneapolis: The University of Minnesota Press, 1960.

Rogers, E. M., *Social Change in Rural Society*. New York: Appleton-Century Crafts, 1960.

Slocum, Walter L., *Agricultural Sociology*. New York: Harper and Brothers Publishers, 1962.

Vidich, Arthur J., and Bensman, Joseph, *Small Town in Mass Society*. Garden City, New York: Doubleday and Company, 1960.

Wileden, A. F., *Rural Community Development*. Madison, Wisconsin: University of Wisconsin Press, 1961.

Religion

Bertram, Robert W., ed., *Theology in the Life of the Church*. Philadelphia, Pennsylvania: Fortress Press, 1963.

Burtness, James, and Kildahl, John, ed., *The New Community in Christ*. Minneapolis, Minnesota: Augsburg Publishing House, 1963.

Elert, Werner, *The Christian Ethos*. Philadelphia, Pennsylvania: Muhlenberg Press, 1957.

Fairchild, R. W., and Wynn, J. C., *Families in the Church: A Protestant Survey*. New York: Association Press, 1961.

Forell, George W., *The Protestant Faith*. Englewood Cliffs, New Jersey: Prentice-Hall, Inc., 1962.

Heiges, Donald R., *The Christian's Calling*, Philadelphia, Pennsylvania: Muhlenberg Press, 1962.

Kraemer, Hendrick, *A Theology of the Laity*. Philadelphia, Pennsylvania: The Westminister Press, 1958.

Marty, Martin E., *Second Chance for American Protestants*. New York: Harper and Row Publishers, Inc., 1963.

Marty, Martin E., *The New Shape of American Religion*. New York: Harper and Brothers Publishers, 1959.

Matson, Theodore E., *Edge of the Edge*. New York: Friendship Press, 1961.

Mattson, A. D., *The Social Responsibility of Christians*. Philadelphia, Pennsylvania: Muhlenberg Press, 1960.

Norden, Rudolph F., *Key to the Full Life*. St. Louis, Missouri: Concordia Publishing House, 1963.